Custom
HARLEY

Custom
HARLEY

Timothy Remus

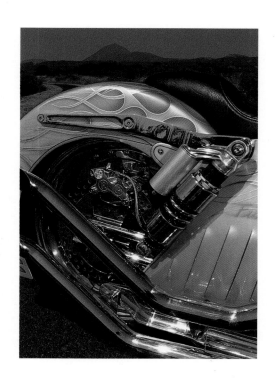

CHARTWELL
BOOKS, INC.

A QUINTET BOOK

Published by Chartwell Books
A Division of Book Sales, Inc.
114 Northfield Avenue
Edison, New Jersey 08837

This edition produced for sale in the U.S.A.,
its territories and dependencies only.

ISBN 0 7858 0938 4

This book was designed and produced by
Quintet Publishing Limited
6 Blundell Street
London N7 9BH

Creative Director: Richard Dewing
Art Director: Clare Reynolds
Designers: Deep Design, James Lawrence
Project Editors: Keith Ryan and Andrew Wilson
Managing Editor: Diana Steedman

Typeset in Great Britain by
Central Southern Typesetters, Eastbourne
Manufactured in Singapore by United Graphic Pte Ltd
Printed in Singapore by Star Standard Industries Pte Ltd

CONTENTS

INTRODUCTION

Acknowledgments

I wish to thank all the bike owners and builders for their cooperation in supplying technical information and for making the machines available for photography. I must also thank Horst Rösler from Frankfurt/Main, Germany; Chris Beattie from Frankston Heights, Australia; and Jeff Hackett from Bridgeport, Connecticut for lending images and material that made it possible to produce a world-class book on custom Harley-Davidsons.

Credit for the photographs can be divided according to which part of the world the bikes came from. European bike photos are by Horst Rösler, while credit for the Australian images must go to *Heavy Duty Magazine*, Australia. Images of the American bikes are my own, with the exception of the Panhead chopper photos seen in Chapter One and supplied by Jeff Hackett.

Timothy S. Remus

CUSTOM HARLEYS – WHY?

What is it about Harley-Davidsons? Even owners of brand new Softails and Dressers feel the burning need to change the bike the engineers in Milwaukee worked so hard to perfect. Improvements might start with just a few little things. Maybe a different seat or a new set of exhaust pipes. Other owners go farther, much farther, until very little of the original machine remains.

These uniquely American machines have been called a "rolling billboard," one that each rider paints to suit his or her individual tastes. Dave Perewitz and Donnie Smith, two of the best-known American customizers, have a unique perspective on this whole business. For nearly 30 years a steady stream of long customized machines have rolled out of the door of their respective shops. If you ask them to identify the motivation that keeps bike owners buying new custom parts and bringing bikes to their shops for customizing, they come up with surprisingly similar answers.

"They want to be an individual," says Dave Perewitz from his shop near Boston, Massachusetts. "These riders want the bike to be a reflection of themselves. The customers I build bikes for give me a lot of freedom in the way I build the motorcycle," says David. "But I spend a lot of time with the person before we start so I understand their tastes. What styles they like or don't like, and *their* favorite colors. Even though I build it, this is their motorcycle."

David's friend Donnie Smith from Minneapolis, Minnesota, cites a similar motivation for the elaborate and often expensive modifications that riders make to their machines. "For most of these riders the bike is an extension of their personality. And I think people like the idea that no two custom bikes are the same, that the bike they build is truly unique."

"People get really involved with their motorcycles" explains Donnie. "It's not like you buy a Chevy T-shirt because you drive a Chevrolet, it's more than that. Maybe because motorcycles are one of the last places where you can feel really free, the machine becomes really important to them."

You might think that after nearly 30 years of building modified motorcycles, the thrill would be gone. For David and Donnie, however, the fire to build another bike better than the last still burns deep inside.

"I like the artistic part, designing the machine, and I also enjoy putting the bike together," says Donnie. "But the best part is when the bike is all done and I can stand back and look it over. Usually they turn out like I imagined. When I see my ideas come together into a finished motorcycle, that's the best part."

"My customers have always been happy with what I build," says David. "But I like some of the bikes better than others. Sometimes I build one that just has *the look*. For me that's the pay back, when I see that *look*."

LOOKING BACK ON THE EARLY DAYS OF CUSTOMIZED HARLEYS, MOST PEOPLE RECALL ONLY THE PSYCHEDELIC IMAGES OF "CHOPPERS" FROM 1969 AND 1970. PANHEADS WITH EXTREMELY LONG SPRINGER FORKS AND METAL-FLAKE GREEN PAINT JOBS. WHAT MANY OF US FORGET IS THE FACT THAT THE CHOPPERS EVOLVED FROM EARLIER MOTORCYCLES, AND THAT THOSE EARLIER BIKES SET THE STAGE FOR THE BIKES WE REMEMBER SO WELL. AN ABSOLUTE STARTING POINT MIGHT BE AN ARBITRARY THING, BUT THE SECOND WORLD WAR MAKES AS GOOD A BEGINNING AS ANY. THOUSANDS OF RETURNING GIS CAME HOME WITH MONEY IN THEIR POCKETS AND BOUGHT MOTORCYCLES. MANY BOUGHT THE SAME BIKE OR BRAND THEY SAW DURING THEIR TIME IN EUROPE. THUS THERE WERE HARLEY-DAVIDSONS ON THE STREETS DURING THE 1950S AND 1960S, BUT THERE WERE ALSO PLENTY OF TRIUMPHS AND BSAs.

ABOVE This old flathead uses foot clutch and a hand shift on the left side of the gas tank.

FAR RIGHT Many of the choppers were Panheads, simply because old Harleys with Panhead engines were relatively common and inexpensive when the boys were looking for a bike to build. Note the kick start and early style air cleaner.

MAIN PICTURE A new bike built to look like a genuine chopper from the 1970s. Note the extended springer fork, extreme rake angle, hardtail frame and Panhead engine. Not all the real choppers looked quite this good.
Photo: Jeff Hackett

Many of those early Triumphs were customized with a smaller gas tank, a trim seat and a "Bates" headlight. The idea was to simplify the bikes, eliminate anything unnecessary, and replace the necessary things like handle bars with parts that had more class.

The Harley owners were doing very similar things to their bikes. Even before the war riders were installing the longest of the factory front fork assemblies, though no one was changing the fork angle at that time. Front fenders were removed and the rear fender was trimmed or bobbed and in the slang of the day these simple pre-choppers were known as "bobbers."

What we call an aftermarket for parts started after the war, when you could buy parts for your bike somewhere other than the local dealer. One of those new stores, the Flanders store in Pasadena, California, offered an extensive line of accessories, including higher, narrower bars and the parts needed to adapt them to then-current Harleys.

Motorcycle slang

The new handle bars went higher and higher until riders were nearly standing up to reach the handle grips. They looked like apes hanging from a tree. Names and slang terms like ape-hangers evolved on the street and became part of the two-wheeled culture.

At the other end of the bike a "sissy bar" gave the passenger a backrest. Veteran bikers say that sissy bars started out as a short handle that could be used to push or pull the bike if you got stuck off-road. Whatever their origins, sissy bars, combined with either ape-hangers or pull-back bars, helped to define the custom bikes being built in the late 1960s and early 1970s. Open any early chopper magazine from the period and what you find is bikes that established a look and style that remains popular to this day.

Harley-Davidson riders started with a "74," essentially a full-size Knuckle or Panhead, and stripped off anything that wasn't essential. Hardtail frames were the order of the day. At the front a long, extended fork supported a 21-inch front wheel.

Riders sat low on the bike with legs stretched out to reach the "forward controls" or highway pegs. A contoured seat provided support for the back and helped the rider become part of the machine. Harleys were considered the best of this breed, though plenty of Triumphs and Hondas were modified with hardtail kits, high bars and extended forks.

Chopper magazines

By the late 1960s and early 1970s motorcyclists of the day had a number of magazines to choose from, each one filled with parts to buy and articles explaining how to install them correctly. Those early magazines carried ads for sissy bars, handle bars and custom seats. The list of available parts was quite extensive and included complete Hardtail frames, extended tubes for "glide" forks, springer fork assemblies and a hundred smaller items.

Even though anyone could construct a bike with new parts, some people developed a reputation for building complete bikes with hand-fabricated parts. Among the feature bikes in the early magazines certain names began to appear with regularity. Men like Arlen Ness, Dave Perewitz and Donnie Smith established themselves as professional custom builders - men who made their living building and selling custom bikes and fabricated parts.

The history of early customizing is well documented by the early magazines. *Street Chopper, Chopper, Big Bike, Modern Cycle, Supercycle* and *Easyriders* began to cover the best of the bikes and carried ads from a hundred new companies both large and small.

A water-stained copy of *Street Chopper* from 1970 features a chopper from San Bernardino, California, equipped with all the right stuff – a "thirty over" fork, 21-inch front rim with Avon tire, blue metal flake paint job, tall sissy bar and a bobbed custom fender.

The movie that inspired the look

If one thing, one event, immortalized "the look" of a long stretched-out motorcycle, it was the movie *Easy Rider*. Peter Fonda's bike set the pattern that is still being followed today: Rake the frame and extend the forks. Design the seat to put the rider down low, add forward controls and a sissy bar. Finish with plenty of chrome and a bright paint job.

Easy Rider captured the look and spirit that riders and builders had been working toward for 20 years. Tom Rudd, founder of the well-known aftermarket company Drag Specialties, remembers the movie well. "The day after that movie opened the phone never stopped ringing. Suddenly everybody wanted a bike like the ones in the movie."

Various motorcycle fads have come and gone since then, but the popularity of that particular look refuses to go away. Just open up your favorite motorcycle magazine and check out the styling of the newest cruisers from Japan. Their look and lines can be traced directly to those early choppers and cruisers of 1969, 1970 and later. Open a copy of any current custom motorcycle magazine – retro choppers are back in fashion, right down to the springer forks and Panhead engines.

The bikes changed through the years. Gas tanks got smaller and forks became longer. Neck angles were altered to 40 and more degrees. The small, Mustang tanks were often molded into the frame. At first the really cool bike was a Knuckle or Panhead. Then Sportsters and finally Panheads and Shovelheads took center stage as the coolest place to start when constructing a chopper.

Nobody left the bikes alone. Riders of the day did much of their own work and bought their parts at the local "chopper shop." Some of those chopper shops were actually fairly sophisticated paint and fabrication facilities run by men working to establish themselves as custom bike builders.

American exports

American riders weren't the only ones craving and building choppers. Europeans, and the Swedish bikers in particular, developed a fondness for long Harley-Davidsons. While the laws in countries like Germany wouldn't allow any radical customizing, the Swedes had more freedom to alter fork angles and install fabricated parts. In fact, when choppers fell from popularity in America in the 1980s, the Swedish builders continued to make choppers. As Frankie from Frankie's Parts in Sweden explained, "Sweden is a very anglo-oriented country. When the long bikes first became popular, they started building them too. When Americans stopped building them, the Swedes they keep going with their own style, so clean and beautiful."

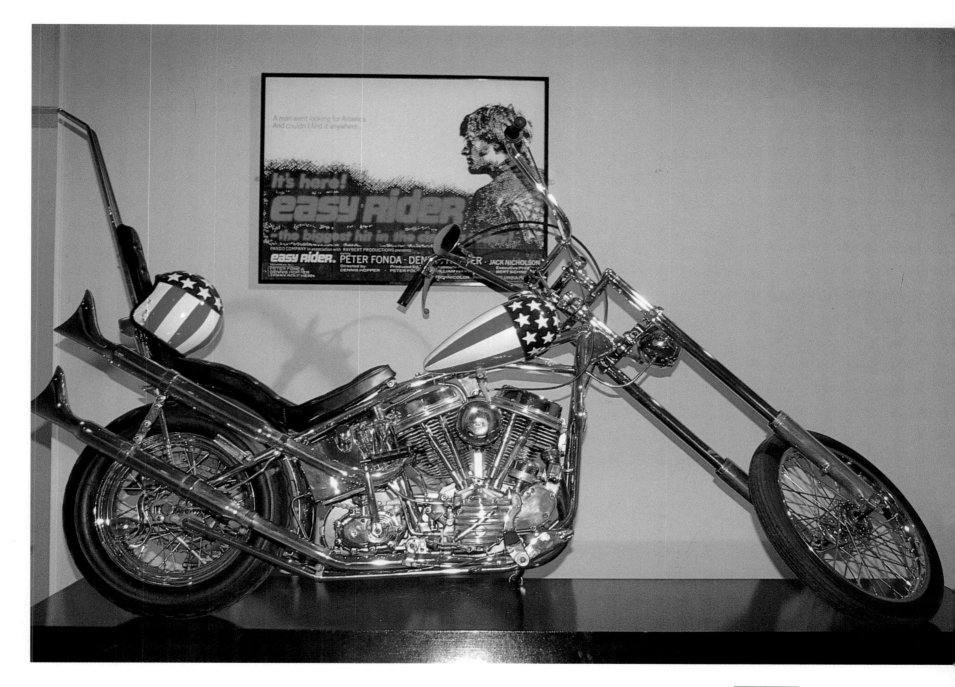

ABOVE As seen at the Barbican Center's Art of the Harley exhibit, this Easy Rider replica was built by Paukis Harley-Davidson in South Germany. More than any other single machine, this bike created the chopper craze, which in turn helped spawn the current passion for custom Harley-Davidsons.
Photo: Horst Rösler

Death of the choppers

By the early 1980s people stopped building the wild custom machines. As the customers stopped building and buying, the chopper shops closed or evolved into normal service facilities.

In retrospect the blame can be laid, at least in part, on the soft American economy at the time. Perhaps because of the economy, motorcycle sales of all kinds took a nose dive at the start of the new decade. The other reason people stopped building bikes was simply because they didn't have to any more. By 1980 you could buy a factory-built custom from Harley-Davidson. A bike with extended forks, more rake, a 21-inch front tire, padded sissy bar and a red-on-black flamed paint job.

The flamed Harley-Davidson Wide Glide from 1980 was only the first in a long line of "custom" bikes built at the Harley-Davidson factory. Milwaukee had, for years, ignored the trends, but starting with the Wide Glide, Harley-Davidson began genetic transfer on a corporate scale.

From Wide Glides the factory quickly moved to the new Softail bikes. By using a triangulated swingarm the new Softail had the look of a Hardtail without the harsh ride. The first true factory cruiser was created by pairing the new pseudo Hardtail frame with more of the California-Classic styling cues seen earlier.

The creation of the Softail and all the models based on that frame was the best marketing move ever made by Harley-Davidson. The Softail chassis serves as the foundation for at least four families of very successful bikes. Before that time Harley had the engine, what could be described as the ultimate American motorcycle powerplant. With the addition of the Softail line, Harley-Davidson had the sound and the look that defines an American motorcycle.

The mid and late 1980s were not a good time for custom bikes or the aftermarket industry. Customizing your bike meant adding a few chrome accessories or possibly repainting the sheet metal. Custom builders kept their operations small in order to survive.

Around 1990 the tide turned and riders began once again to make an individual statement with their motorcycles. Each year since 1990 has been better than the last, with more new bikes sold, more people wanting to improve their bikes and more offerings from the aftermarket.

Though the young riders have aged, each one still needs a Harley and each of these machines needs to be different from all the rest.

People wait for two or three years to get a new Harley. Once they own the bike the stock sheet metal comes off, replaced by new parts and fresh wild paint schemes.

Milwaukee is working hard to meet the demand for bikes. At the same time they're introducing new custom parts and accessories to compete with the huge aftermarket. Farther down the line the small custom shops are looking for larger facilities and more fabricators.

Each of the best-known customizers has forged a relationship with a large aftermarket corporation. Rick Doss works with Custom Chrome while Don Hotop designs for Drag Specialties. In addition to their work with the best-known builders, each of these companies buys designs on a case by case basis from freelance fabricators and designers. Nearly all the companies maintain good relations with the King of American customizing, Arlen Ness; who with help from his son Cory puts out hundreds of new trendsetting parts each year.

A nice feature of these relationships is the fact that most Rick Doss or Don Hotop designs are sold under their own label. Thus the new exhaust pipes in the catalog are listed as a "Rick Doss" custom part or "Don Hotop" design.

This corporate recognition seems an affirmation of the important role these individuals play in a very healthy industry. Without them there might not be four or five major companies selling everything from taildragger fenders to billet aluminum running boards. They set the styles, create something for all the riders to shoot for - and provide proof that it can be done.

European bikes and bikers

Europeans have always ridden motorcycles, more recently they've discovered Harleys and custom Harley-Davidsons in particular. When the Barbican Gallery in London put together an exhibit called "The Art of the Harley" in early 1998, they brought in customized Harleys from both America and various European countries. English, German, French and Swedish builders contributed to the exhibit with a variety of designs: everything from brutally fast German bikes to the long extended shapes of the Swedish choppers.

Each country has its own style, dictated partly by taste and partly by regulation. German laws are strict, and the bikes tend to reflect that with alterations that are more conservative than those found on other European bikes. The Swedes build choppers for the 1990s, and the French create elaborate flowing designs painted in bright colors.

Setting the record straight

New riders from either continent, astride their first Sportster or Softail, tend to think this whole phenomena is new, that Rick Doss or Arlen Ness have only just started designing bikes, that people are only now beginning to rake the frame to push the front wheel out ahead of the bike.

However, the best-known designers and the busiest shops all have roots that date back to the 1960s and earlier. In fact, the whole wave of success being enjoyed by both Harley-Davidson and the aftermarket can be traced back to those exciting days of yesteryear. Unable to leave their machines alone, those first fabricators set the stage for a phenomenon none of them could have foreseen at the time. Customized Harley-Davidsons have become both a craze and an industry. The passion to create a personal motorcycle burns across boundaries, transcending language and culture. It has, in fact, become an entire culture in itself.

ABOVE Two of Arlen's earliest surviving motorcycles, a Shovelhead and a Sportster. Note the struts, wild paint and handle bars on the Sportster, and the overall simplicity of both machines.

KING OF THE
CUSTOMIZERS
ARLEN NESS

ABOVE From short stubby choppers to very long, flowing "Aero" motorcycles like this one, Arlen is never short of new concepts. Built on a prototype rubber-mount softail-style chassis, this aero bike also uses the new billet aluminum engine covers with the soft radiused shapes.

RIGHT After more than 30 years as a prolific bike builder, Arlen Ness never seems to run out of new ideas.

Arlen Ness and his wife Bev opened their first store in San Leandro, California in 1970. From that early 200 square foot start, Arlen has progressed until now, almost 30 years later, he reigns as the undisputed king of custom Harleys. In many ways, Arlen's history runs parallel to the history of customizing. He has affected and been affected by that history so thoroughly that it's hard to tell one story without telling the other.

Arlen built his early reputation on innovative paint jobs. The small store was only open in the evenings and functioned primarily as a way to stop customers from constantly coming to his house to drop off or pick up parts. Hanging on the shop wall were a few custom parts and chrome-plated accessories. One of Arlen's big turning points came shortly after opening the store when he created a unique set of "ram horn" handle bars for his own bike. The bars were a great success and soon Arlen and Bev had people lined up outside the store to buy a set of Arlen Ness handle bars.

Arlen Ness became part of the motorcycle aftermarket, providing would-be customizers with the unique parts necessary to build a custom bike of their own. As time went by Arlen added more handle bar designs, struts to replace the shock absorbers, complete springer fork assemblies and various sheet metal parts. Coverage of Arlen's bikes in magazines like *Custom Chopper* helped build name recognition for both Arlen and his emerging line of parts.

Ten years later Arlen and Bev moved to a larger store. It is interesting to note that during the time the custom Harley market was sliding into the doldrums, Arlen continued to build bikes for both himself and his customers. While many shops were closing or scaling back their operations, Arlen was able to show modest growth. That growth left him well positioned when the world of custom Harleys started its renaissance in the early 1990s. The rebirth of the V-twin sent people scrambling for new ideas and parts. Many of those bikers and builders found the Arlen Ness store in San Leandro.

One visitor was the new owner of Drag Specialties. After being let down a hundred times by people who "evaluated" his parts by sending them to Taiwan for manufacture there, Arlen forged his first good relationship with a large aftermarket catalog company.

In addition to the licensing agreements he signed with Drag, Arlen continued to add parts to his own direct mail catalog. About the same time Arlen took on a new part-time employee destined to go far, a certain young man named Cory Ness. Cory gradually worked his way up through the organization until today he is responsible for all day to day operations as well as future planning. The current success of Arlen Ness Incorporated, with distribution not only in the States but in Europe and Japan as well, is due largely to Cory's involvement.

Today all the major catalogs feature Arlen's parts, and every major magazine carries ads. Like the industry in general, Arlen is doing better today than he could ever have imagined. And like the industry, the roots of that success go back 30 years and more.

The bikes

A Knucklehead was Arlen's first ride and first custom Harley, but during the early years of the 1970s he built many Sportsters as well. Most of these bikes contained a new front frame section, fork, and sheet metal. When Arlen was finished, very little of the original bike remained. Never afraid to go his own way, Arlen turned away from the super-long choppers of the day and started building bikes that were low and lean, "diggers" in the slang of the day.

Ness bikes have always had a certain style, a look all their own, as well as a host of mechanical innovations. With help from chassis builder Jim Davis, Arlen was able to create long frames from small-diameter chrome-moly tubing. Sheet metal fabricator Bob Monroe helped Arlen create his own unique fenders and gas tanks, often with hidden oil tanks that routed the oil through the frame instead of through conventional oil lines.

In 1979, Arlen's newest bike, Two Bad, debuted in the custom bike magazines. Built around two Sportster engines set in a Jim Davis fabricated frame, Two Bad forever set Arlen apart from the other bike customizers of the day. Throughout the 1980s Arlen continued to produce wonderful works of mechanical art, including his Blown Shovelhead and Nesstique, a Sportster with the antique styling.

If Nesstique looked old and spindly, Arlen's Ferrari Bike looked modern, fast and massive. Another of Arlen's "major bikes" the Ferrari machine utilized two blowers, four carburetors, and Testarossa styling cues.

One of Arlen's major strengths is his ability to shift gears in a design sense. After building the sleek and flowing Ferrari bike, he decided to build a chopper "like they used to be," complete with a wild overlapping flamed paint job. The first chopper was so well received that Arlen continues to build a few each year. Some have the old Panhead engine while others have been built with Shovelhead or Evolution engines.

If Arlen was one of the first to turn away from the super-long choppers, he was also the first to embrace the idea of rubber mounting the engine. Arlen pioneered the long-low-cafe look for FXR Model Harley-Davidsons when they first came out and went on to build his own rubber-mount chassis. The current and very popular Luxury Liners are based on his second generation rubber-mount chassis.

As if that wasn't enough, he's also in the middle of building a few early-style Sportsters in his own frame, many of them with sidecars! And, of course, there are those other stray bikes, like the long red "Aero" bike that looks like it should be in a museum, the Bugatti bike he built a couple of years ago, the aluminum bike with the overhead camshaft motor, and plans for a dozen more.

Arlen Ness, the bike designer who never stops learning, creating or building motorcycles, each one more interesting than the last.

LEFT This Arlen Ness chopper is actually part of a series of bikes, each essentially the same with differing details. Like all good choppers this one rides on a hardtail frame and uses a springer fork up front. And like an early chopper (not the ones we remember from the magazines and movies) this one comes without any additional rake or an extended fork.

ABOVE Arlen has a knack for building bikes that make people smile, like this immensely popular '57 Chevy bike.

LEFT Arlen's Ferrari bike is another of his larger-than-life motorcycles. A massive 128-cubic-inch V-twin force fed by two superchargers and four carburetors, set into a hardtail frame and covered with some very interesting sheet metal.

HARLEY-DAVIDSON CUSTOMS COME IN EVERY SIZE, SHAPE AND COLOR IMAGINABLE. FROM 883CC SPORTSTERS TO MONSTER-MOTOR SOFTAILS. FROM BIKES THAT RELY ON AFTERMARKET FRAMES TO THOSE THAT USE A STOCK FXR CHASSIS. BECAUSE OF THE ENORMOUS VARIETY OF HARLEY-DAVIDSON CUSTOMS, THE MACHINES DON'T ALWAYS FIT INTO NEAT CATEGORIES. ELSEWHERE THIS BOOK IS GROUPED LOGICALLY, BUT THIS CHAPTER IS FOR MACHINES THAT DIDN'T FIT ELSEWHERE – LIKE THE SOFTAIL WITH SO MUCH ONE-OFF EQUIPMENT THAT IT DOESN'T FIT IN THE SOFTAIL CHAPTER, AND THE TWO FXR BIKES THAT WE'VE CALLED A MILD CUSTOM INSTEAD OF RUBBER-MOUNT BIKES. OR THE ARLEN NESS BIKE WITH THE OVERHEAD CAM ENGINE THAT USES AN FXR-STYLE RUBBER MOUNT-ING SYSTEM. OR THE EUROPEAN BIKES: NEITHER IS A SOFTAIL AND BOTH BOLT THE ENGINE RIGIDLY TO THE FRAME. YOU GET THE IDEA. THINK OF THIS CHAPTER AS A VARIETY PACK WITH A TASTY NEW SURPRISE ON EVERY PAGE!

ABOVE Cylinders show evidence of polishing, hexing and painting. Nifty coil bracket is from Dave Perewitz with CompuFire coils. Sportster rocker boxes give the engine a different look.

LEFT Paul's FXR is built around molded factory sheet metal, nice paint and mild graphics. Air dam is the only piece of non-stock sheet metal.

AN FXR
BUILT TO BOOGIE

Everyone has their favorite Harley. Some like Softails for their looks while others want to cruise in style: Dresser style. Paul Shadley from Whitman, Massachusetts, is an FXR man, "I like the way they drive and the fact that they don't vibrate. The way the engine and transmission are rubber mounted, that's a good system."

When Paul bought his "new" 1988 FXR it was, in his own words, "really hideous." So hideous he could only stand to ride the beast for a few hundred miles before pulling it apart for a complete rebuild and paint job. He and brother Mark own Auto Tec, an automotive repair facility. Though they work hard during the day, they reserve evenings and Saturdays for the really important jobs like motorcycle projects.

Thus it was one Saturday morning when Paul started to pull apart his new FXR. Off came the sheet metal, out came the motor and transmission. Paul kept turning Allen bolts in a counter-clockwise direction until the FXR was reduced to a bare frame surrounded by fenders, wheels and assorted parts.

Paul likes to do most of his own work, yet some parts of the FXR rebuild went to outside craftsmen with special talents. The bottom end of the 80-cubic-inch V-twin was rebuilt and balanced by Jim Thompson from Dedham, Massachusetts. Paul's brother Mark ported the Harley heads and installed the new black diamond valves and Jim Thompson valve springs. South Shore Plating polished the cylinders and heads before Auto Tec painted the cases and the areas between the fins.

With the cases and bottom end finished Paul installed a stout EV 59 Camshaft from Andrews with .560 inches of lift. Next he installed new high-compression Wiseco pistons followed by the polished and painted "ten-over" cylinders. The ported heads and adjustable push rods were next, topped off with chrome-plated Sportster rocker boxes. Near the end of the engine project Paul installed the polished Mikuni carburetor, Compu-fire ignition and Perewitz/Sullivan billet coil bracket and coils.

Paul hates to do things by halves, so he completely disassembled the five-speed transmission and replaced the stock gears with back-cut cogs from Andrews. Externally the transmission was treated much like the engine, with a painted case and a billet Perewitz top cover.

The current trend is for custom bikes with enormous rear tires, lowered so far they drag the frame on driveways and any kind of corner. Paul explains that he has a different attitude when it comes to lowering the bike. "I like to ride hard," explains Paul. " And I knew this bike would be ridden two-up, so it's only about one inch lower than a stock FXR. We have a rule of thumb at the shop, you should be able to slide a beer can under the frame, if you can't then there isn't enough ground clearance."

The factory 39mm narrow-glide forks have been rebuilt with new seals, Works springs and damper tubes from Progressive Suspension. A pair of Koni shocks, one inch lower than stock, provide good handling and bring the back end of the bike down to match the height of the front. The frame itself is nearly stock. "We did a modest wedge-rake," explains Paul. "We added five degrees to the fork angle, and then we molded all the rough areas on the frame."

The deep red paint seen on Paul's new ride is kandy brandywine from House of Kolor. Nancy Brooks did the simple silver graphics, which are buried under a series of clearcoats.

Like the disassembly, Paul began the final reassembly on a Saturday morning at the Auto Tec shop. For brakes he chose GMA four-piston calipers and master cylinders, with one in front and another at the back. The rest of the wheel and brake hardware comes from the Sullivan/Perewitz partnership. The polished rotors and rear belt pulley all match the design of the Desperado billet wheels. The rear wheel measures 16 inches and carries a 140 series Avon tire. The front tire, another Avon, this one stamped 90/90X19, surrounds a Desperado billet wheel. The sheet metal Paul bolted in place is very similar to the stock sheet metal he took off, with the addition of a Sportster taillight molded into the back fender.

The road test of Paul's new FXR came in Sturgis, South Dakota. On the freeway the new FXR provided a smooth, vibration-free ride. The combination of compression, camshaft, carburetor and Bub pipes provided more than adequate power all the way to speeds that would have a highway patrol car hard pressed to catch up. But it was in the canyons where the new machine really shined. Anyone who wondered why Paul didn't lower the bike farther found out first hand on the twisty roads to Deadwood. Suddenly they were left looking at the small Sportster taillight disappearing around the next curve.

BELOW The taillight is an early Harley light molded into the fender. Stock swingarm uses upgraded aftermarket hardware for the axle mounting, adjusting and the pivots.

GOOD PARTS MAKE
A GREAT MOTORCYCLE

When Clayton Shepard from Anoka, Minnesota, set out to build a motorcycle, he didn't want a radical ride. Which is not to say that Clayton stinted on the project. Clayton chose to build a high-quality machine by combining the talents of Donnie Smith, the famous customizer, with a good basic design and some high-grade hardware and parts.

The project started as an accident bike that Clayton bought with Donnie's help. "We knew from the outset that this was going to be a project bike," explains Donnie. "As soon as it came into the shop we pulled it apart."

Once apart, the FXR frame received a mild rake job, but no additional stretch. Seven additional degrees seemed plenty, just enough to place the front wheel in front of the bike. The rest of the changes that Donnie and his team made to the frame are more subtle.

The area under the seat, the signature triangular area, contains a number of small changes. Under the side covers the triangle has been paneled in. The side covers themselves look stock at first, until you take a second look. As Donnie explains, "We took two side covers for each side and made one longer cover. Normally the covers fit inside the tubes, these new ones reach out and overlap the tubes slightly. It makes that area seem longer and stretches out the whole bike."

Another change is the oil tank. The standard FXR tank extends out from under the seat until it almost reaches the rear cylinder. By crafting a taller oil tank with the same capacity, but no bulge, Donnie "opens up" this area and give the bike a lighter feel. Other frame work includes the molding done by brother Greg and the addition of new shock absorber mounting points on the stock swingarm.

Like the frame changes, most of the stock sheet metal was massaged and used again. The front fender is minus the rivets that used to hold it together and the gas tank with the small Donnie Smith gas cap fits the frame much better than did the original. At the back, the early-style taillight is now an integral part of the fender and the license plate sits on a slanted bracket above the taillight. The only totally new piece of sheet metal is the small air dam located behind the front wheel, a nice accent created by Rob Roehl.

The chassis hardware is a combination of modified Harley-Davidson parts and high-grade components from the aftermarket. The stock Showa fork with the 39mm forks is still there, holding up the front wheel, though now the frame sits two inches lower than it did before. What didn't come from Harley-Davidson is the four-piston calipers with the PM logo milled into their surface, or the floating rotors on either side of the Sturgis 19 inch aluminum wheel.

LEFT Deep purple used on cases and cylinders complements the magenta paint seen on the sheet metal. Even the inner primary, coils and the center part of the rocker boxes are painted in the purple hue.

Brake and wheel hardware at the back matches that used in front, though of course the wheel measures 16 inches in diameter and mounts a 150 series Avon tire that Donnie somehow squeezed into the space normally filled by a 130 tire.

The engine follows the same theme, a combination of modified original parts and very high quality aftermarket components. Local engine builder Lee Wickstrom from Shakopee, Minnesota, completely disassembled the engine, and then sent the cases and cylinders out for polishing and powder coating. Following a careful inspection, Lee balanced the stock flywheel assembly and then reassembled the lower end with new bearings. Next, he filled the Harley cylinders with S&S high-compression pistons, topped off with complete S&S cylinder heads.

Working in harmony with the high-performance heads, Lee recommended a 561 camshaft and the Super G carburetor, both from S&S. To round out the breathing part of the engine package, Lee and Clayton chose a set of Python pipes from Drag Specialties.

The five-speed transmission is filled with back-cut gears for easier shifting, all housed in a polished case with a chrome top cover and a billet ART side cover that houses the hydraulic slave cylinder.

The magenta paint from House of Kolor is the work of Jerry Scherer while the subtle graphics are by Craig Smith. The rest of the hardware continues the quality theme seen throughout the bike: Arlen Ness bars with billet grips and a small speedo and tachometer from Drag Specialties.

A good engine makes power because all parts work together in mechanical harmony. Likewise, a nice custom motorcycle achieves its appeal, not because of one part, but because all the parts and pieces work to create a certain visual impact. Together, Clayton, Donnie and all the rest used good parts to build a great motorcycle.

ABOVE Small mechanical speedometer and electronic tachometer from Drag Specialties are mounted on a chrome plated bracket bolted to the handle bar risers.

LEFT This FXR exhibits a certain synergy. The basically good design is enhanced through a long series of seemingly minor changes and upgrades.

NO REGARD
FOR BORDERS

ABOVE A traditional bike with Shovelhead engine, springer fork and ape-hanger bars, with innovative side covers, billet wheels and even billet floorboards.
Horst Rösler.

Built across national borders, Fabreeze is testimony to the fact that the love of motorcycles, Harleys in particular, knows no bounds. Fabrice Roux, owner of Fabreeze is also the publisher of *Freeway*, the well-known French custom-bike magazine. When it came time to upgrade his personal ride, he asked Rikki at Battistinis in Bournemouth, England, if his shop could apply their flair for wild flowing custom bikes to his personal FXE.

Battistinis started by cleaning up the front of the frame and molding all the factory welds. It's in the sheet metal though where the

Battistini knack for design is most evident. The one-piece gas tank with twin fillers is a Battistini original, as are the elaborate louvered side covers that enclose the oil tank and extend down to the frame and back to the shock absorbers.

Battistinis has for some years now enjoyed a good relationship with Arlen Ness and some of the parts on this bike come from the Ness catalog. The taildragger rear fender, for example, is from Arlen, as are the flamed grips and billet floorboards.

The wheels, measuring 21 inches in front and 18 at the back, are from another well-known American company, Performance Machine, as are the four-piston calipers used on both the front and rear of the bike.

An extremely short pair of reservoir shock absorbers connect the twin rail Arlen Ness swingarm to the Harley-Davidson frame. Up front

the suspension comes by way of the Paughco chrome-plated springer fork assembly. Apparently a bike with a springer fork needs ape-hanger bars, no matter which country the owner calls home.

In the United States we consider Evolution engines as the only viable V-twin powerplant. Europeans have a more open mind. When Rikki asked how far to go with the motor, Fabrice answered, "All the way." Outside, the cases, cylinders and heads received a thorough polishing job. Inside, the cylinders received a clean-up bore and new Harley pistons, new bearings for the bottom end, and new valves for the Shovelheads. A Crane cam opens the valves while a Series E carburetor from S&S mixes the fuel. Exhaust is handled by another American product, the wild upswept pipes from Custom Chrome.

The stock four-speed transmission bolts to the frame just behind the engine, though it too received the polish, paint and rebuild routine used for the engine. A primary belt connects engine and transmission, hidden behind the ribbed and polished aluminum primary cover.

The very complex paint job with overlapping flames is the work of an American painter, Jeff McCann. Jeff used lacquer paints from House of Kolor to create the tangerine layout with lime green flames and fuchsia highlights. Another American, Danny Gray, made up the special seat to Rikki's order.

An Arlen Ness air cleaner, FuB forward controls and hand made switch panel for the left side round out the parts and accessories used to complete the final assembly of this international creation.

Horst Rösler from Germany, the man who does freelance work for *Freeway* (including the shots of this bike), summed up the bike pretty well when he described it as "a combination of the Battistini style combined with the French taste for extraordinary customs."

TOP LEFT 18-inch PM rim is supported by the Arlen Ness swingarm. Shovelheads were built in the days when most bikes used chain drive to the rear wheel. Fabricated chain guard matches the design of the switch panel. *Photo:Horst Rösler.*

ABOVE Not many of the original Shovelheads came with an air cleaner like this one. Note the cam cover and the flamed kick start lever.

FRENCH FINESSE
FOR A GERMAN CUSTOM

CENTER TOP Massive swingarm is built to accommodate a wide 190X17-inch tire, but something had to give - there is no room for belt drive.

BELOW This German machine combines a large displacement V-twin with an aftermarket frame and sheet metal. *Horst Rösler.*

Built by the Legend bike shop in Schellebelle, Belgium, this Orange Evo-powered custom combines the best attributes of both German and French bike builders. As Horst Rösler from Germany explains, "This bike combines French stylish paintwork with the German knack for very powerful engines."

The hot engine in this Legendary bike comes from a 97-cubic-inch engine based on Sputhe cases and cylinders capped by Edelbrock heads. Inside the polished cases and cylinders is an S&S 4-1/4 inch flywheel assembly and 3-13/16 inch Sputhe pistons. Gas and air enter the big bore brute via a Mikuni carburetor each time the Crane cam opens an intake valve. Spark comes with help from a Crane HI-4 ignition and the spent gas and air exit via the Carbon Dream pipes.

A stock primary chain takes the considerable power of the Sputhe engine to a set of five-speed gears housed in a Softail-style transmission housing. Even though the bike is not a Softail, the engine and transmission mount to the frame directly, as they do in a Softail frame (unlike the bikes with "rubber-mount" engines).

The frame from Custom Framesale in Holland is manufactured from mild steel tubing with five inches of stretch and a 36-degree fork angle. The fork itself is a high-performance upside-down design from

W.P. in Holland, supporting a three-spoke aluminum wheel. The wheels used on this bike are an interesting choice for two reasons. First, they measure 17 inches in diameter, an uncommon size for a Harley custom. Second, they come not from the aftermarket, but from a Suzuki sport bike.

The twin four-piston brake calipers used at the front come from the same Suzuki, as does the single caliper and rotor combination used on the rear wheel. And while some modern Harleys use belt final drive, this one uses a chain between the transmission and rear wheel, partly to make room for the 190/80X17-inch Metzeler rear tire mounted on another donor aluminum rim.

The rear wheel is supported by the fabricated swingarm machined from a solid piece of 6061 aluminum. The same raw material is used for the unique rear fender struts and even the bracket used to support the carbon fiber muffler.

Custom Framesale supplied the very modern front fender and the more traditional rear fender. The same crew fabricated a one-piece gas tank and the custom-fit oil tank located just below the seat. The paint color is midnight orange, sprayed in acrylic lacquer, with airbrush graphics applied on top of the orange and then buried under a series of clearcoats.

Though the bike contains very few parts from Harley-Davidson, it is indeed a very colorful "custom Harley." A unique blend of hand fabricated parts, German engineering and French design.

CENTER BOTTOM Front and rear brakes come from a donor Suzuki, mounted here with a fabricated bracket. Carbon fiber muffler subtracts from the weight while adding to its appeal.

BELOW Sputhe cylinders and engine cases are made from their own Nitralloy aluminum alloy for maximum strength. Cylinders are cast around a steel liner so it becomes an integral part of the cylinders.

A 'CAMMER FROM ARLEN

This is a story about an engine, as much as a motorcycle. It gives us another opportunity to look at Arlen Ness; his curiosity and his knack for borrowing ideas from outside the normal ranks of custom Harleys and using those ideas to continually present us with new designs and concepts.

The bike shown here contains one of the first Arlen Ness overhead cam engines. The idea of placing the camshafts above the valves isn't new. Racing motorcycles and cars have used the design since the 1920s. Production automobiles have used single and double overhead cams for more than 30 years. However, this technology was never applied to the standard Harley Big Twin engine, until now.

Enter Arlen Ness, who by chance met an innovative machinist, a man who had already designed several overhead camshaft kits for the small-block Chevy V-8. It didn't take long for Arlen to ask if a similar conversion could be done for the all American V-twin.

The design dispenses with the conventional cam, pushrods, lifters, rocker arms and rocker boxes. Instead, a single camshaft, supported by an aluminum housing, bolts onto each head. In addition to the camshaft, each of these housings contains two roller rocker arms supported by their own shafts. A crank-driven gear, located where the camshaft once lived, turns the two camshafts through a toothed belt.

In a standard pushrod engine the valve springs have to close the valve as the cam lobe rolls past the high point. In doing so they have to work against the inertia of all the valve-train parts. Pushrods and tappets get heavy at high RPM, especially on an engine with long pushrods and relatively large roller tappets.

Because the new overhead cam design eliminates most of those heavy valve-train parts, the heads can be assembled with lighter valve springs. According to Arlen, the results of all these improvements were evident right away. Even the first test bike cranked over without the typical Harley grunt and seemed to pick up revs faster than most V-twins.

That first test bike worked so well that Arlen and the boys rode it for some time before disassembling the engine for a good inspection. Once apart, everything looked so good they ordered three more prototype kits and installed one on the bike Cory Ness rode, without incident, all the way from California to Sturgis, South Dakota.

With the new valve gear the engines revved much more quickly and easily, though the redline had to remain rather conservative due to the basic internal dimensions of a stock V-twin. With a bore of $3\text{-}1/2$ inches and a stroke of $4\text{-}1/4$ inches these are never going to be 7,000 RPM engines, no matter how sophisticated the valve gear is.

Arlen thought it would be interesting to bolt the overhead cam kit onto an engine with different bore and stroke dimensions, one that could take better advantage of the overhead design. A discussion with S&S, the largest aftermarket supplier of V-twin engines, produced an engine based on a set of their big-bore cases designed for a 4-inch bore. By mating these to a crankshaft with a 4-inch stroke, they created a "square" engine.

Thus Arlen paired his new overhead cam kit with the S&S 100-cubic-inch engine. The net result is an engine that combines a large total displacement with the ability to reach relatively high RPM.

LEFT More than just a custom motorcycle with an innovative engine, Arlen's red Racer is a bike built on new ideas. Note the fenders, headlight, air dam, gas tank and exhaust pipes.

ABOVE Normally the boring side of a V-twin engine, you can see how the front exhaust pipe makes a U-turn to run across the left side of the polished and painted cylinders. Vertical member behind the seat and the tubes that form the seat areas have been radically altered to get the seat so low. Oil tank is located under the transmission.

A special engine needs a special chassis. In this case, it's an Arlen Ness FXR-style chassis with some serious modifications. First, the frame is modified near the back to dramatically drop the seat height. And instead of using one of his standard dual-rail swingers, Arlen put together a triangulated swingarm that looks like something from a radical softail-style chassis. The shock absorbers are supported by the frame immediately behind the seat, making for an almost horizontal mounting position. The special shock absorbers are from Fournales and use high-pressure air in place of the standard spring.

The unusual swingarm leaves room for a 180X18-inch Metzeler tire and belt drive. Mounted outboard of the drive pulley is the large-diameter brake rotor and below that the four-piston brake caliper, all part of Arlen and Cory's new left side rear brake assembly.

The front fork assembly uses sliding axle supports so the ride height is adjustable over a wide range. The tubes themselves mount to radiused billet mid-glide triple trees. Dual disc brakes with new six-piston calipers slow down the front wheel, which is covered by a very brief fender with billet supports. The rear fender is bobbed, much like the front, and uses similar aluminum supports.

Though the exhaust pipes run down the right side in typical fashion, the routing is rather unique. The pipe for the front cylinder-head makes a sharp left turn and runs across the left side of the engine before crossing over again to run side by side with the other pipe. The unique routing prevents any kind of interference, literally or visually, between the pipe and the trick drive system for the overhead camshafts.

Arlen's long time friend "The Mun" did much of the fabrication on this bike including the turn-down gas tank and the unusual front air dam. The molding on the frame and sheet metal parts is the work of Jesse Diaz while the paint and graphics come from Brouhad Design.

Many of Arlen's bikes aren't just custom motorcycles. They're rolling test beds for new ideas and untried designs.

Arlen has once again collected a whole series of new shapes and designs and assembled them all into a running motorcycle. The frame, swingarm, headlight and fenders represent potential new products for Arlen. Yet, these shapes and designs are more than that. They represent a large influx of new ideas and fresh energy into the world of customized Harley-Davidsons. The kind of energy and ideas that keeps an industry, an entire phenomenon, fresh and exciting.

ABOVE A single belt drives both camshafts from a gear located behind the "cam cover". Carburetor is a Shorty from S&S with a velocity stack instead of an air cleaner.

ABOVE·LEFT Unusual fork assembly allows Arlen to raise or lower the front of the bike without disassembling the fork. Note the large-diameter rotors and Arlen Ness calipers.

ABOVE Nearly all the parts on Jesse's new bike were fabricated by hand. To describe this as a softail-style custom doesn't really do it justice.

OFF THE SCALE

Some bikes are nice, some are awesome and a very few are off the scale. The red "Softail" seen here definitely falls into the *off the scale* category. Built by Jesse James, owner of West Coast Choppers, the red bike catches your eye when first seen from across the parking lot at a crowded event. Like a truly good design, this motorcycle looks even better when you cross the parking lot for a better look.

Bending over to check out the curved rear fender struts you realize that there's a neat little polished support for the front fender that

uses that same tapered shape in miniature. After further examination you realize there aren't many parts here that look familiar. It turns out that most of the machine was fabricated by Jesse, a member of his crew, or an outside subcontractor.

The frame was built in-house. Instead of using solid steel vertical side plates under the seat, Jesse used concave "half tubing" bent into a curve. The rear fender is supported by similar material, which arches and tapers as it runs to the end of the fender. Many of the parts on the bike create a question in the viewer's mind – *How did they do that?*

Gordon Rooth, a fabricator in Jesse's shop, started with two of their own "blanks" to create the tapered rear fender and the very

trim and graceful front fender. The gas tank is Jesse's own. He fabricated the whole thing from scratch using a sheet of raw aluminum. Which might not sound too impressive until you realize that there are only a handful of tin-benders in the country who can pull off such a task. The oil tank, a perfect fit for the frame, is another example of Jesse's talents.

The unusual wheels are one-off designs, carved on a very large CNC machine from a big chunk of billet aluminum, big enough that the rims are an integral part of the spokes. The front rim measures 19 inches in diameter and relies on a slim, trim Jesse James fork assembly for support. At the back a 180x18-inch Metzeler wraps a

ABOVE The unique air cleaner, gas tank and exhaust pipes were all fabricated for this one machine.

ABOVE The Fender Man, Jesse James, a man on his way up.

RIGHT Low profile 18 inch tires used on both ends work well with the overall design of the bike. One-off wheels exhibit a great shape, matched by the brake rotors.

OPPOSITE The engine too is an unusual piece. The cylinders and heads with the very precise looking fins are billet aluminum pieces from Patrick Racing.

matching rim and spoke combination. A single four-piston Performance Machine brake caliper mounts at either end. The rotors, which don't look like anything from the PM catalog, are apparently two more "Jesse James" originals.

The only piece Jesse didn't fabricate is the polished V-twin, though even that is almost a one-off piece. The cases and 4-$\frac{1}{4}$ inch S&S flywheel assembly might be common enough, but the 3-$\frac{1}{2}$ inch Patrick Racing billet cylinders and matching heads aren't what you would call commonplace. The hand formed aluminum air cleaner protects a Super G carburetor from S&S while a pair of fabricated exhaust pipes run down along the bottom frame rail.

There is only one color for machines such as this. Damon's Painting applied the redder than red hue to the frame, fenders, tank and even the headlight shell. "Koon" did most of the final assembly, which included running the wiring inside the frame, and installation of the fabricated bars and grips.

Rumors persist that one motorcycle "clone builder" was so taken with the shape that he bought the rights to the design. Under this scenario, Jesse would build the basic machines, in limited numbers, and then ship them to another facility for finishing. Maybe by the time you read this it will be possible to buy an off-the-scale bike for yourself – without hiring an entire crew of fabricators.

AS THE WORLD AROUND US CHANGES AT A FASTER AND FASTER RATE, IT IS REASSURING TO CONSIDER THE SPORTSTER. FIRST INTRODUCED IN 1957 AS THE XL (BASICALLY AN IMPROVEMENT ON THE EARLIER, FLATHEAD K BIKES) THE SPORTSTER STILL CARRIES THE SAME NAME AND EVEN THE SAME ESSENTIAL LOOK THAT IT DID OVER FORTY YEARS AGO.

INTRODUCED ORIGINALLY AS A "SPORTY" HARLEY-DAVIDSON, THE SPORTSTER WENT FROM EARLY SUPERBIKE TO CHEAP HARLEY, TO A WOMAN'S BIKE, BUT RECENTLY IT SEEMS TO BE RETURNING WITH MORE OF THAT ORIGINAL SPORTY INTENT. THROUGH IT ALL THE ORIGINAL DESIGN HAS REMAINED INTACT. A BASIC MACHINE WITH ONLY TWO CYLINDERS FED BY ONE CARBURETOR. NO PLASTIC PANELS OR NEON GREEN GRAPHICS. JUST ENOUGH MACHINERY TO GET YOU DOWN THE ROAD WITH A CERTAIN RESERVED STYLE.

THOUGH THERE ARE HUNDREDS OF THOUSANDS OF SPORTSTERS ON THE STREET, A REALLY NICE CUSTOMIZED SPORTSTER STILL SEEMS A RARITY.

THE CATALOG EMPIRES ALL OFFER MORE AND MORE PARTS, AND PLENTY OF THOSE ARE DESIGNED FOR THE XL FRAME. PERHAPS BY THE TIME AN ENTHUSIAST IS READY TO CREATE A WILD BIKE OF THEIR OWN, THEY'VE MADE THE MOVE TO A BIG TWIN.

PRESENTED HERE IS AN OVERVIEW OF STREET BIKES – FROM A FABRICATED CAFE RACER TO A LIGHT TOURING MACHINE. FROM A GERMAN ROAD RACER TO A "MODERNIZED" LATE MODEL SPORTSTER. BECAUSE THEY ARE UNCOMMON, THESE SPORTSTERS TAKE ON SPECIAL SIGNIFICANCE. THESE AREN'T JUST CUSTOMIZED HARLEYS, THESE ARE CUSTOMIZED HARLEY-DAVIDSON SPORTSTERS.

ABOVE RIGHT Larger tank with two fillers mimics the look of the classic Fat Bob tank.

RIGHT Cocked and ready to ride, this is one Sportster many people would mistake for a Big Twin.

FAR RIGHT Left side of the bike shows the early style round horn, the forward control for the shifter and the battery behind the chrome cover under the seat.

A BIKE OF HER OWN

In the wind, Jean on her very nice "first bike."

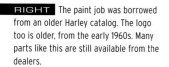

The paint job was borrowed from an older Harley catalog. The logo too is older, from the early 1960s. Many parts like this are still available from the dealers.

Most new Harley owners buy a bike and ride it for a period of time before making any major changes. Jean Engebretson from Duluth, Minnesota, did it differently. She ordered a new Sportster at the same time as her husband, Wade, ordered a Fat Boy. They both waited patiently for delivery, and when Jean's Sportster came in first she decided to have it customized before bringing it home.

"It isn't that I don't like the way the Sportsters look," explains Jean, "but they all look the same. I wanted this bike to be unique, I wanted it to be my very own. So that's why I decided to have it customized as soon as it came in."

Jean explains that the basic idea for the bike came from a photo she saw in a magazine. "There was a Sportster there with the same front fender, that's where the whole thing started. The other big idea came from an old Harley-Davidson brochure. There was a 1967 Harley in the brochure with the same basic two-tone paint job we used. The early emblem on the tank dates from 1962."

The new skirted front fender and Fat Bob-style tank came from the Custom Chrome catalog and both are designed to fit the late-model Sportster chassis. Most of the work on the bike was done by Marty and the crew at the Sport Center. For the paint work, however, the boys at the dealership sent the sheet metal to Scott McTavish at Gene's Auto Body in Duluth. Scott used Harley-Davidson paint, a candy red on top and birch white on the lower part of the gas tank.

Scott explained that the work is so time consuming that he usually ends up doing it in his own time in the evenings and weekends. "People don't believe it," says Scott, "but I ended up with almost 40 hours of labor in the preparation and paint for Jean's Sportster."

Jean says that when they started modifying the bike there was what she calls a certain "rebounding" effect. "The bike evolved. We did one thing and then we'd have to do something else or it wouldn't look right. We did that until the budget was gone."

The new gas tank for example meant Jean needed a new speedometer as well. The crew at the Sport Center installed a Harley-Davidson speedometer and ignition switch. The mini light bar used to relocate the rear turn signals is from Custom Chrome, however, as is the lay-down license plate bracket. Instead of the stock seat, Jean elected to use a fringed solo seat from Mike Corbin. To make sure there would be room to stretch out on the highway a set of forward controls from Custom Chrome were added.

Some of the changes to Jean's ride are more subtle than the sheet metal, though no less important in the long run. The large front turn signals for example were discarded and replaced by unobtrusive oval accessory lights mounted just below the switch assembly on either side. In order to provide Jean with some storage space a pair of Harley-Davidson leather saddle bags were added to the rear. The combination of Fat Bob-style tank, saddle bags and two-tone paint scheme all work to give the Sportster the look of an early Big Twin.

To really lock in that look of a bigger bike from an earlier time period, Jean and the boys added just a few more accents. At the front, for example, there's the chrome-plated engine guard. Between the cylinders on the left side is the antique style horn from Harley-Davidson. And in place of the stock rectangular mirrors are the round mirrors, also from Harley-Davidson.

You can hardly have a custom Harley these days without having it lowered. In the case of Jean's bike a pair of shortened shocks brings the rear of her bike down a full two inches. The front fork was shortened the same amount with a factory low-suspension fork kit.

When it came to the engine, Jean's budget was spent. So she opted for turn-out mufflers and left everything else alone. If you ask her though, she says an engine upgrade to 1,200cc is next on her list of things to do.

But for now Jean is happy. When she's not riding with her husband Wade, alongside his Fat Boy, she's on a weekend ride with a local group called the Ramblin' Roses.

In all the time she's spent out with other club members or at the local motorcycle watering holes, Jean has seen plenty of Harleys and late model Sportsters. However, one thing she hasn't seen in all these travels – is another Sportster with a skirted front fender, Fat Bob tanks and a great two-tone paint job. Which makes Jean the owner of a unique Sportster, a bike that really is her very own.

THE ABILITY TO SEE

Architects look at a bare piece of land and envision a finished building. Interior designers walk into a house of bare white walls and imagine what it will look like with just the right wallpaper, furniture and drapes. Call it imagination or call it vision, it is the ability to look at a piece of coal and see a bright sparkling diamond. When Lynn Mattis looked at a certain 1986 Sportster he didn't see the cafe-ized Sportster with the low bars in need of engine work. Instead he saw a much different motorcycle. One in perfect shape with great paint and a strong engine.

Lynn's wife, however, did not share his enthusiasm for the new bike. "When my wife gave me a ride over to pick up the bike she didn't get it. She couldn't understand why I was buying the bike. She likes motorcycles, but she just couldn't see past the bike in front of her."

Lynn bought the bike anyway and drove it home to his somewhat typical suburban Minneapolis house. The only thing non-typical about Lynn's house is the neighbors – he has bikers living across the street. In fact one of those is an especially notorious biker by the name of Donnie Smith.

"Donnie and I have been friends for years and we made this deal," explains Lynn. "He agreed to do the metal work and the chassis modifications and I would bolt everything together in my own shop."

About the time Lynn began the disassembly his friend Dave Roehl (better known locally as Frog) volunteered to do the paint work. So with the excellent team of Donnie Smith for fabrication and Frog for molding and painting Lynn proceeded to strip the Sportster down to its bare bones.

Donnie's bike surgery included not only the neck and swingarm but also the more subtle work done for cosmetic reasons. In order to run a wider rear tire, Donnie suggested an FXR rear fender, modified in this case to accept a '41 Chevy Taillight and supported by fabricated struts. Instead of a Sportster gas tank he recommended a Sport Bob tank from a company in California. Though the tank came with two gas caps there was only one, placed in the center, when the tank was finished. The final piece of cosmetic work came in the form of a one-piece battery and ignition cover for the left side.

Frog eliminated any lingering scars and it is his careful "plastic surgery" that gives the frame its clean lines and the tank and fenders their smooth surface. With the plastic work finished Frog applied the single-stage metallic green paint and then waited for John Parks to do the graphics before applying the final clearcoats.

The engine already displaced 1,200cc and breathed through heads with enlarged valves, so Lee Wickstrom from Kokesh M-C only needed to install a new crankshaft assembly and a set of Andrews V4 camshafts. The Super E carb that came with the bike was left in place while a pair of Python pipes were added as a good compromise between traditional looks and good performance.

RIGHT Aftermarket tank has been converted to a single filler with a slightly raised rib along the top. Sportster engine displaces 1200cc.

While Lee had the engine apart Lynn gathered up the engine covers and sent them out for chrome plating. All except the center rings of the rocker box set, which were painted green to match the rest of the machine. During the disassembly the cylinders were painted black though the heads were bead blasted and left in raw aluminum.

Lynn was a little overwhelmed when all the parts came back to his garage. "I spent a lot of nights sitting in the garage with all these parts lying on the floor. It took a while but I just went at it one part at a time until it started to look like a motorcycle again. Another of Lynn's little improvements is the spoked wheels used in place of the cast originals. Gary at Kokesh M-C laced up the 19 inch front and 16 inch wheels with chrome rims and twisted spokes for extra sparkle.

The seat is from Keith Nybo who created the modern profile seen here, built on the seat pan supplied by Donnie Smith. Because of the stretched swingarm the new seat mounts farther back than the original and provides Lynn with more room to stretch out his arms and legs.

When the bike finally came together everyone thought it looked great, even Lynn's wife Durene. Though green is a somewhat uncommon color for Harley-Davidsons Lynn stands by his color choice. "It's a good color for the bike, and it even provided the name that I use for the bike, *Green Go*."

Lynn succeeded in building a very nice, clean Sportster because he could see beyond the obvious. Instead of worrying about what the Sportster looked like he focused on something else – the ability to see a longer, greener and sportier Sportster.

ABOVE LEFT Lynn used chrome in moderation. Air cleaner is painted, as is the oil tank.

LEFT By enclosing the battery and ignition module under one fabricated cover, the bike takes on cleaner lines.

RIGHT Not a radical ride, but a long way from the cafe-Sportster Lynn originally purchased.

A FLAT TRACK XR
BUILT FOR THE STREET

From this angle it's easy to see the "Sportster" in this XR. Rear fender is a fabricated unit with an early Harley-Davidson taillight.

Larry Page of Richmond, Virginia, is a man who loves motorcycles. Among his collection is a '47 Knuckle and a '49 Pan, as well as a few modern customs. But if you told Larry he could have only one motorcycle, it would be this XR 1000. "I'm a flat track fanatic," explains Larry. "I go to the races all the time. In fact, I used to sponsor a rider a few years back."

Now flat track bikes like race-ready XR 750s, are few and far between. So Larry set his sights on a more modest prize, an XR 1000 street bike. This personalized XR was never actually for sale. It didn't even appear at all. As Larry tells the story, it all started with an engine. "I was in Daytona during Bike Week a few years back looking for a bike to buy. Somehow we were at this machine shop and there was an XR 1000 motor for sale. The engine was complete, packed into a box, the carburetors and everything."

It didn't take long for Larry to close the deal and pack the engine back home to Virginia. Next he found a frame, in the form of a late model Sportster frame that had been "chopped up a little bit" but was otherwise sound.

A motor and a frame may be the essence of a motorcycle, but Larry was still a long way from having a running XR 1000. While he looked for more parts, the motor was shipped to Departure Bike Works in Richmond, Virginia, where it was pulled apart for a complete inspection. What they found put a smile on Larry's face: an engine in very good condition. The heads had already received some port work, and everything else looked to be in good shape. Departure's job then was to freshen the internals and brighten the externals, with polished covers and heads, and bright stainless steel fasteners.

To complete the chassis, Larry bought a 43mm Ceriani fork assembly from Storz and a pair of short, Progressive shock absorbers for the rear of his new bike. While he was looking through the Storz catalog he spied the alloy, one-piece gas tank, which seemed the perfect choice for his competition-inspired XR. Harder to find was the

special oil tank, with the recess to clear the rear carburetor. A factory tank was finally located on a dealer's shelf.

About the time all the parts came in from Storz, Larry realized that he wasn't making much progress on the new bike. Outside help seemed the logical answer and he turned to Randy at Milwaukee Iron in Lynchburg, Virginia.

Randy and his crew started by cleaning up and repairing the damage to the old Sportster frame. The metal men at Milwaukee Iron left the frame with stock rake and stretch dimensions, but modified the short stubby tubes at the very back of the frame. Instead of mounting the fender strut, the frame stub was trimmed and extended to blend into the fender and support it without the need for a strut. To eliminate those ugly bolt heads, the new un-strut was tapped so the fender bolts could be screwed in from the backside.

At the other end of the frame Randy couldn't find any triple trees that he liked, so he fabricated a pair of mid-glide trees from 6061 aluminum. In keeping with the performance theme, a pair of four-piston calipers from PM were bolted to the front lower legs. At the

back, another PM, four-piston caliper squeezes another ventilated, polished rotor.

Rather than use the more traditional 19 and 16 inch wheels and tires, this XR carries 18 inch Avon rubber at both ends. The Avon tires mount on light 18 inch aluminum wheels from Performance Machine.

The Storz-supplied flat-track gas tank forms the center piece of the simplified sheet metal for Larry's modified XR. The minimalist fenders, fabricated by Milwaukee Iron, might not keep off much rain, but the style fits the rest of this bare-bones bike. At the very back an early-style Harley-Davidson taillight is molded into the fender itself. The solo seat is another one-off item, this time from the able hands of Danny Gray. When all the parts were finished the frame and sheet metal were shipped to Keith Saunders for the bright orange and white paint job.

After six months of searching for parts and fabricating the ones that couldn't be found, Milwaukee Iron was finally able to assemble all the pieces into a running bike. For an exhaust system they used a set of SuperTrapp pipes from Storz. The handle bars are flat-track style with just a little lift and integral risers. Instead of being rear-set, the brake and shift levers are located in their standard Sportster location for easier around-town riding. Though it took him a long time, Larry Page finally got his flat track bike.

ABOVE Storz supplied the SuperTrapp exhaust for the left side, as well as the dirt track-inspired gas tank.

ABOVE LEFT In the best racing tradition this bike uses a Ceriani 43mm fork assembly, dual four-piston Performance Machine brake calipers, and a very trim front fender. Wheels measure 18 inches on either end.

A STREET LEGAL
ROAD RACER

Europeans are developing a taste, not only for Harley-Davidsons, but for Harley-Davidson racing. This competition takes the form of both – All Harley Drag Racing and the 883cc Cup road racing series popular in Britain and France.

The Milwaukee Racing Center, located in Oberthal, Germany, is in the business of transforming stock Harleys into more aggressive, powerful and roadworthy motorcycles. Hans Jürgen Boujong, owner of the Race Center, sells the full line of parts from WiWo, a well-known German company that designs and sells high-performance parts for both race track and street use.

Hans and crew built a bike that definitely puts the Sport back in Sportster. While the low and slow crowd slam their Big Twins right to the ground for boulevard cruising or stoplight racing, this Sportster sits high and dry to maximize clearance on the corners.

The stock rear shocks (due to be replaced with some high-quality aftermarket shocks) bolt to the rather substantial WiWo swingarm with the eccentric axle adjusters. The adjusters are used to tension the belt that runs to the rear pulley. The pulley itself bolts to an innovative WiWo disc wheel. The modular design allows the owner to change the rim at a later date, without buying an entire new wheel

and hub assembly. The wheel in question is 17 inches in diameter, matched to a 3-$\frac{1}{2}$ inch rim, wide enough to support the Bridgestone 140X17-inch tire.

The front suspension is equally normal, at least when viewed from a "custom" perspective. The WiWo inverted front fork uses air in place of springs to support the bike. Aluminum triple trees, again from WiWo, mount the fork assembly to the frame. The disc-style front wheel bolts to an aluminum rim with an 18 inch diameter coupled with a Bridgestone tire.

The brakes for this street-legal road racer are made up of standard, high-performance components, like the single WiWo four-piston caliper and 330mm rotor used on the front wheel. The somewhat less

important rear brake uses another four-piston caliper mated to a smaller, 230mm rotor.

Hans considered the performance of the 1200cc Sportster engine to be more than adequate and replaced only the carburetor, with a Series E from S&S, and the exhaust with the dirt track pipes from SuperTrapp.

Though the emphasis here is on the hardware and the parts that make the machine a more precise two-wheeled bullet, the not-so-hard components are interesting too. The front fender, for example, is a collaboration between Hans and the people at WiWo. The trim shape is made from carbon fiber to be both light and durable. The gas tank is from Zodiac, a "Fat Bob" design intended to fit Sportster frames.

ABOVE The SuperTrapp mufflers are tunable, both the noise level and the engine's output can be modified according to how many discs are used at the end of each muffler.

ABOVE LEFT The WiWo wheels have a number of advantages, light weight and high strength are primary. They also allow the owner to change rim sizes without changing hub or disc.

ABOVE The German-built
Sportster sits high, the better to allow
plenty of clearance when carving
through the countryside at high speed.
Horst Rösler.

The rear fender and seat combination comes from the crew at the Racing Center.

Not only can they fabricate and assemble a complete motorcycle, Hans's crew can paint as well. Even the graphics are the work of the talented hands at MRC.

Relatively flat Sportster bars on short risers point the way, with both speedometer and tachometer mounted dead center to tell you how fast you're getting there. Grips on either end and the mirrors are all from Arlen Ness and the rear-set brake and shift levers provide the proper "cafe" seating position.

The Milwaukee Racing Center customized this road-race Sportster, though they didn't really create a custom Harley in the conventional sense. What they built instead is a faster, more corner-friendly motorcycle. A road-race bike built for the street, one good enough to compete daily in the real-world Grand Prix.

Stock Sportster tanks aren't known for their capacity. This Quick Bob tank holds more gas and gives the bike a very different look.

NOT JUST ANOTHER "CR"

In 1977 Harley-Davidson introduced a radical new model, the XLCR Sportster. The "CR" stood for Cafe Racer and the model came with an extended tank, small fairing and abbreviated rear fender. At the time of its introduction, the bike was seen as too different and despite Willie G's best intentions, sales of the new cafe racer were very disappointing. Time, however, alters our collective opinion. Now, more than 20 years after its introduction, the XLCR has gone from ugly duckling to collectible classic.

Bob Heinze of Minneapolis, Minnesota, always liked the CR Sportsters. He thought about buying a CR, but they all had "collectible" price tags - and they were all exactly the same. There was only one thing to do, Bob decided to build his own, slightly different, Sportster CR.

Bob started with a 1977 Sportster and the help of his friend Donnie Smith. Following a complete disassembly, Donnie stretched the frame four inches and raked the neck an additional five degrees. Once the top tube was extended, Donnie and Bob could bolt on a genuine XLCR gas tank - an essential part of the conversion to Sportster CR. Rather than try to find a factory tail section, Bob found an old fiberglass chopper fender and "night light" taillight assembly. The look is similar to that of a factory CR, yet unique to this motorcycle.

At the front of the bike Bob used a cafe-style fairing and small fender from the Arlen Ness catalog, to mimic the look of the factory CRs. Mounted inside the fairing is a simple gauge set with tachometer and speedo, both from Drag Specialties

Even after finding and modifying most of the sheet metal, there were still plenty of parts to find and modify. Bob used a 1979 Sportster swingarm, so he could easily mount disc brakes and a late-model cast wheel. That meant moving the lower shock mount forward to match the shock mounting on the earlier frame. The shocks themselves are shorter than stock, to lower the back of the bike roughly three inches. While they were doing all this work the swingarm was "bridged" for strength and then sent off to the chrome-plating shop.

The front suspension is based on the original Sportster fork, cut two inches. The small PM calipers are mounted to the fender mounting points with special Donnie Smith brackets, coupled with polished, drilled rotors.

Bob thought that his new Sportster should have something extra in the horsepower department and turned to Eagle Engineering of Minneapolis for help. The crew at Eagle recommended more cubic inches, in the form of a stroker bottom end and a stock bore.

This combination created a 74-cubic-inch street engine. To make the most of that, Eagle ported the Harley heads and installed four high-lift camshafts. Behind the classic S&S teardrop air filter sits a Super E fuel mixer also from S&S.

How the motor looks in a custom bike is almost as important as how it runs. Bob went all the way and had the cases, cylinder fins and heads polished to a high luster. To create pipes similar to those used on the CRs Donnie started with 1979 Sportster pipes. He then modified these so the pipes run together from the point where they meet to the single collector mounted on the right side. While factory pipes were black, Bob's shine with chrome plating.

Near the end of the project Bob needed just a few more things to pull everything together. The hand-fabricated oil tank is the work of Donnie Smith, as is the small chain guard and the bracket for the PM rear brake caliper. For a custom seat Bob called on the talents of upholstery wizard Keith Nybo while Rick Haugland did the great flamed paint job.

Bob's Sportster gets plenty of attention whenever he stops. Some people think it's one of those "Harley cafe racers." Until they look closer and realize that it's something much more interesting than a *stock* XLCR.

ABOVE This bike is a combination of off-the-shelf parts and hand-fabricated hardware. Front fairing and fender are from Arlen Ness, gas tank is from Harley-Davidson. Unique oil tank, fender struts and exhaust were built by Donnie Smith.

49

ABOVE The unique gas tank is a factory CR item. This is actually the second tank. The first was mounted solid to the bike and developed cracks due to vibration. Underneath all the shine is a 74-cubic-inch iron-head engine with a stroker bottom end, ported heads and S&S carburetor.

ABOVE RIGHT Front half of the exhaust is made up from a set of Sportster pipes combined with the double pipe fabricated section leading to the small collector.

RIGHT On the other side of the rear wheel (Sportsters put the chain or belt on the right) is the fabricated chain guard and the plated sprocket. Note the nice hardware used for the axle and even the chain guard.

BILL'S LITTLE PROJECT

The story of Patty's blue Sportster started when her late husband Bill Mesenbrink saw an Evolution Sportster at the local Harley store. Bill liked the bike, not for himself, he thought it would be a great bike for Patty. At the time Patty was riding an Ironhead Sportster and Bill figured it was time she stepped up to the new generation of Sportsters.

"Bill convinced me that I needed the bike," recalls Patty, "and that with just a little work we could have it fixed up to be a real nice bike." Like so many of these real-life stories, the project took a *little* more work than Bill expected.

As Patty remembers it, looking back, "We were just going to take off the sheet metal, get the bike repainted, and maybe re-chrome some of the covers because the chrome was pitted. Then one night I

ABOVE Chrome plated lower legs are mounted in billet aluminum narrow-glide triple trees.

ABOVE RIGHT In the wind, Patty Mesenbrink on her very unique Sportster.

came out into the garage and Bill had the whole thing ripped apart."

Bill was always handy with a set of wrenches, but sometimes it helps to have additional resources. People who might have more expertise in customizing and painting than you do. In Bill and Patty's case, they had two old friends who would prove very useful in fixing up the old Sportster - bike-builder Donnie Smith, and custom-painter Jon Kosmoski.

Bill took the frame to Donnie so the neck could be raked an additional five degrees and thus give the bike a little more of what Donnie calls "attitude." Donnie also created the one-piece battery and ignition cover on the left side. The rest of the sheet metal parts came from the Custom Chrome catalog, including the fenders and the Quick-Bob gas tank. The sheet metal parts and the gas tank in particular are designed to give a Sportster a bit of that "Big Twin" bulk.

At the time Bill and Patty were building this Sportster Jon Kosmoski had virtually retired from active painting and was spending most of his time running House of Kolor, his paint manufacturing

company. But Patty asked her friend and Jon agreed to paint the bike and even the wheels, which involves a lot of extra taping.

Jon painted the sheet metal with kandy oriental blue sprayed over a blue metallic base. With design ideas provided by Patty he also painted the multi-colored graphics and then buried everything under a series of clearcoats. Before Jon could tape and paint the factory wheels, Bill took them to a machine shop in Minneapolis where the rim area was cleaned up and polished for a bright shine.

The used Sportster Patty bought at the dealer was the "base model." The one with the small engine, no radio and no air conditioning. Small in this case is a 883cc V-twin that can best be described as an engine with a lot of potential.

The good news is the ease with which the small engine can be bored out and equipped with a 1200cc kit. At 1200cc most Sportster motors realize enough potential to give Big Twins a run for their money. Dewey's M.C. in Minneapolis bored out Bill and Patty's cylinders to the new 1200 dimension and also ported the heads to flow more air. Reassembly included a set of Andrews camshafts and a

Crane HI-4 ignition. Along the way Bill took most of the engine parts over to his friend Frog's house where they carefully prepped the aluminum and applied the purple paint. Another friend, Pat Obinger, contributed his polishing and plating expertise by re-chroming the engine covers for both sides of the engine.

Reassembly chores fell to Bill with moral support from Patty. In addition to putting the bike back together, Bill and Patty decided on a few additions. "I didn't want a stripped down bike, I wanted a bike you could use on a daily basis," explains Patty.

If the project was more work than originally planned, it has also been more rewarding than Patty could have predicted.

Patty's Sportster makes a useful daily ride and a nice mini touring rig on the highway. The 1200 kit means more power. Her "little Harley" can keep up and occasionally embarrass the other bikes and bikers she rides with. And the nice paint and unusual sheet metal mean that Patty gets questions and compliments every time she stops for gas.

It turned out to be more than just Bill's little project, but it's also more than just a re-painted Sportster.

ABOVE Single speedometer and no tachometer. Handle bars with a bit of rise make for a nice comfortable seating position.

ABOVE LEFT People are always asking Patty if the engine is powder coated. The answer is no, the purple is just plain old urethane paint applied by Bill and his friend "Frog."

HARDTAILS HAVE ALWAYS BEEN POPULAR WITH A HARDCORE GROUP OF HARLEY ENTHUSIASTS. RIDERS WHO REMEMBER THE WAY IT USED TO BE. THE FIRST BOBBERS WERE BUILT ON A HARDTAIL CHASSIS, BECAUSE THAT'S ALL THERE WAS (REAR SUSPENSION DIDN'T ARRIVE ON BIG TWINS UNTIL THE INTRODUCTION OF THE DUO-GLIDE IN 1958).

CHOPPERS, TOO, WERE BUILT MOSTLY WITH HARDTAIL FRAMES. FRAMES WITH SHOCK ABSORBERS WERE CONVERTED TO HARDTAIL-FORM BY REPLACING THE REAR SHOCKS WITH SOLID STRUTS.

TODAY THERE'S A NEW STYLE OF HARDTAIL, NOT NOSTALGIA CHOPPERS, BUT RATHER MACHINES THAT CAPTURE THE ESSENTIAL SPARK OF MOTORCYCLING.

HARDTAILS BRING RIDERS BACK TO THE BARE ESSENTIALS OF RIDING. EACH HARDTAIL CONTAINS TWO WHEELS, ONE ENGINE, GAS TANK(S), AND MINIMAL CONTROLS. NO REAR SUSPENSION, NO FANCY DASH, NO FULL-COVERAGE FENDERS.

AS THE SOFTAILS AND RUBBER-MOUNTS BECOME MORE MODERN, SOPHISTICATED, COSTLY, AND COMMON,

AN INCREASING NUMBER OF RIDERS ARE TURNING THE OTHER WAY. TO THE BIKES THAT STARTED THE WHOLE PHENOMENA. THEY MAY BE HARD ON YOUR BEHIND, AND LEAVE YOU WITH NO ROOM TO PACK A JACKET, BUT THAT'S THE WHOLE POINT. WITHOUT ALL THE EXTRAS YOU'RE LEFT WITH THE REAL THING, AN UNDILUTED TWO-WHEELED RUSH.

WHAT FOLLOWS IS A LOOK AT FIVE HARDTAILS, ALL ASSEMBLED IN THE PAST FEW YEARS. FOUR ARE BUILT BY PROFESSIONALS WHILE ONE COMES FROM THE GARAGE OF AN AMATEUR CUSTOMIZER. WHAT ALL THE BIKES HAVE IN COMMON IS THAT CERTAIN HOT ROD FLAVOR, A FEELING THAT THEY WERE "STRIPPED DOWN TO GO FAST," AND THAT ESSENTIAL SPIRIT THAT LIVES IN ALL MOTORCYCLES, BUT IS MUCH EASIER TO FIND IN THESE VERY BASIC MACHINES.

RIGHT Right side view shows off the billet wheels, smooth fork assembly and dual carburetors hanging out in the breeze. Note the large-diameter headlight, nitrous bottle and the oil cooler on the left side frame rail.

FAR RIGHT The unique exhaust pipes are the work of Steve Stonez, the same man who crafted the wrap-around side covers. The unique non-chrome plating on the pipes is HPC coating. The small protruding chrome plug is the "passenger foot peg."

MAIN PICTURE Rear fender from Jesse James is located with fabricated, arched fender struts. Under the fender is a low profile 180/55x18-inch tire from Avon. Both the 70 tooth pulley and matching wheel are from Perewitz/Sullivan.

BIKES

THE ESSENTIAL
V-TWIN MOTORCYCLE

I f you ask Terry McConnell from Tulsa, Oklahoma, how he built the little silver hardtail, he makes it sound too easy. "We ordered the parts," says Terry, "and did a mock-up. Then we tore it apart, had the parts painted and put it all back together again."

Terry's account leaves out significant parts of the story. Things like the sketches he did to ensure that the finished bike looked exactly like the idea he had in his mind. Or the careful selection of the right parts to achieve the correct finished effect. There's also the choice of outside fabricators, people who can match the design and do the work on time. And Terry left out the final assembly, which can hardly be described as just "bolting it all back together again."

In the case of this silver machine, Terry started with an idea for a simple bike, nice and light, with clean lines and no extra parts. A hardtail seemed the only answer so Terry ordered a frame from Atlas with three inches of stretch and a 38-degree fork angle. During the mock-up stage a pair of fenders from Jesse James were clamped in place. The way the front fender wrapped close to the tire provided a certain appeal. At the back, a short fender was turned around and trimmed until it looked like it belonged on the emerging hardtail.

BELOW Up front it's another 18 inch Avon tire and Perewitz/Sullivan wheel. New from Perewitz/Sullivan is the fork assembly with the ultra smooth lower legs.

The wraparound side cover is the work of an outside fabricator, Steve Stonez from Stonez Bonez in Tulsa. Steve made the panel from sheet steel according to the sketches provided by Terry, and also made the seat pan. For a gas tank Terry chose a stretched model from Fat Catz. The tank is listed as a model with a five-inch stretch, which allowed Terry to mount it forward on the chassis and still have it come back far enough to meet the small custom seat.

After the mocked-up bike sat on the hoist long enough for Terry to know he had the right lines, it all came apart one last time. The frame and sheet metal parts made their way to the paint shop where the "Dough Boy" (aka Troy Elliot) applied the silver pearl paint over a gray basecoat. At the same time any parts that needed to be polished or plated went to Dave "Thurstin" Howell at Howell Racing.

When the time came to decide on an engine, Terry thought he needed something hot, in keeping with the hot-rod hardtail theme. Yet, as he explains, "I didn't want a monster motor and I didn't want a real expensive piece with lots of billet covers."

The engine Terry installed is based on a stock Harley-Davidson V-twin, with the addition of Wiseco 10.5 to 1 pistons, a Crane cam and

LEFT In the wind, Terry and Tina McConnell on their latest creation.

BELOW Left side of the engine shows off the open primary (part of every proper hardtail), the solenoids for the nitrous and the hand-built pod for the ignition and starter switch.

ported Harley heads. Two Edelbrock QuickSilver carburetors hang out into the airstream on the right side, and are fed gas from the stretched tank and nitrous oxide from the small tank bolted to the downtube.

A belt primary drive, contained in an open billet housing, transfers the engine's power to a five-speed transmission filled with Andrews gears. Another belt runs from the transmission to the rear wheel, this one a stock drive belt connected to a 70-tooth billet rear sprocket. The 70-tooth sprocket and both billet wheels come from the partnership of Dave Perewitz and Bobby Sullivan.

Front and rear rims measure 18 inches in diameter and both mount Avon tires, a 130/70X18 up front and a 180/55X18 in the rear. A single front rotor, designed to match the design of the wheels, mounts to the left side, coupled to a four-piston caliper from Performance Machine. At the back there's another matching rotor and one more four-piston caliper.

A bare bones bike with an attitude, Terry's hardtail goes to show that sometimes when you delete the rear suspension, elaborate paint job and expensive billet parts, you end up with more, not less. More of what might be called the essential V-twin motorcycle.

SECOND GENERATION
BAR HOPPERS FROM BOB MCKAY

Bob McKay from Shallow Lake, Ontario, considers himself both a franchised Harley-Davidson dealer and a custom bike builder. As Bob is fond of saying, "I was a custom builder long before I became a dealer." Among all the different types of bikes Bob has built over the years he especially enjoyed the simple little hardtails. "I'd forgotten how much fun those bikes are to ride, until a customer brought one in that I built 15 years ago. The bike was in really good shape and when the deal was done I took it out for a ride. Nowadays every one is riding Softails, FXRs or Baggers, it was great to get on this light little bar hopper."

There was only one problem with Bob's machine, "The bike was old technology," says Bob. "Panhead engine, chain drive and kick start. So I thought, what if I built one of these with new technology."

The Hog Bike

The first of Bob's new/old hardtails borrows much from those old bikes he remembers so well. The frame is an Edlunds hardtail chassis from Pat Kennedy, with the look of a straight-leg frame from about 1957. This new frame is, however, designed to accept a late-model drive train.

To keep the project cheap, Bob used many "take off" parts he found in the shop. The brakes, for example, were left over when a new-bike customer replaced the stock calipers with four-piston replacements.

The Evo engine is pretty much a stock 80-inch unit, made up of more recycled parts. The cases were damaged factory cases that Bob had repaired. The jugs, heads and nearly everything else are more parts left from other people's upgrades. The only exceptions are the Screamin' Eagle cam and the unique Bob McKay drag pipes.

For a front fork Bob combined shortened 41mm tubes, stock lower legs and White Brothers springs. Arlen Ness triple trees mount the tubes to the frame in Wide Glide fashion and flat drag bars point the way. For a rear tire Bob mounted a 140X16-inch Avon tire on a stock spoked rim while in front he installed a 21-inch Metzeler on another spoked rim from Harley-Davidson.

The project's original goals ruled out the use of anything but simple sheet metal. The only deviation from that rule is the gas tank. Though it is a three-and-a-quarter gallon Sportster tank, the installation of the tachometer into the gas tank makes it a less-than simple highlight to the rest of the bike.

If the tank is too fancy the rear fender is as simple as possible, a flat "Bob Job" supported by a welded strut. Between the tank and the fender is the small seat from Drag Specialties and below that is a McKay-special horseshoe-shaped oil tank.

A basic bike calls out for black paint and Bob understood that fact when he applied the black urethane. Bevin Finlay from Belmore, Ontario is the man responsible for the hot-rod hog on the tank, done before Bob applied the clearcoat.

When Bob took the bike to Daytona, he discovered that not only was it fun to ride, but that other riders would walk past a group of costly Softails just to come and look over his simple little bar bike.

A more modern old hardtail

The red hardtail is decidedly more modern than the little hog bike - evolution for Bob McKay's Evolution hardtails. Like the earlier bike this one comes with no front fender and only the simplest of rear fenders.

If the piggy bike was built on a budget to be very simple, this red bike was built with more money and more flash. Instead of using take-off parts, most of the components used on this machine might be called the best that the aftermarket has to offer.

The V-twin engine displaces a full 96 cubic inches. Not only is this one more powerful than the near-stock 80-cubic-inch motor, it's also adorned with an abundance of aluminum jewelry. The rocker boxes, camshaft cover, transmission cover and left-side primary cover all come from the Arlen Ness catalog, carved from billet aluminum and chrome-plated for maximum brilliance.

What Bob calls "new technology parts" include the brakes, which are made up of billet four-piston calipers from RevTech, two in front and two at the back. And though the earliest hardtails ran springer forks, this red rocket uses a modern hydraulic fork assembly from Arlen Ness. The fancy fork assembly supports a 21 inch spoked rim, while at the back a new 16 inch rim mounts a new Avon tire that measures more than seven inches across.

In the end Bob's two bikes are a unique mix of old and new. The hog bike more old and less new, the sleek red bike, the reverse. Yet, both are part of the less-is-more idea conceived so many years ago and still very viable today.

ABOVE Bob McKay aboard his red hardtail near Sturgis, South Dakota.

OPPOSITE Bob used a Sportster tank, just like in the old days. Except that this one has a very high-performance pig airbrushed on either side, and a tachometer mounted right into the tank.

NEXT PAGE A hardtail for the next millennium? This red bike uses all the fancy parts the black one didn't. The end result is a brighter, more modern, more expensive motorcycle.

AUSTRALIAN SHOVELHEAD EATS EVOS

Most Harley-Davidson riders would agree that the newer Evolution motor is more efficient and faster than the older Shovelhead. Yet, there's an exception to every rule and that exception can be seen here. This "Harman" Shovelhead eats Evos as appetizers and then goes looking for something really tasty, perhaps something served on a bed of rice like a nice Kawasaki or Honda.

What looks at first like just another rigid old Harley is in fact a larger-than-life Shovelhead. A bike that combines John Harman engine components in a custom frame, all of it assembled by Neville Sharp of Melbourne, Australia.

All the pieces that make up the John Harman engine are designed for maximum displacement. The cylinders feature a full 4.325 inch bore and bolt to special reinforced engine cases. The oversize heads

BELOW The front end of this hardtail is simple and effective. Wide Glide fork assembly is borrowed from a Harley Dresser. Each lower leg mounts a four piston caliper mated to a large diameter floating rotor. Nineteen inch wheel assembly is made up of an aluminum rim and stainless spokes.

RIGHT Left side shows off the billet engine cases and fabricated inner primary and belt cover. Belt drive is a 3-inch unit from Primo combined with an Atlas clutch assembly. Note the oil filter mounted between the drive and driven pulleys.

FAR RIGHT Gas tank with Sportster profile, combined with the rigid frame and Shovelhead engine, gives the bike the look of an early-chopper. Note the coils hidden up under the gas tank (each cylinder head contains two spark plugs) and the QuickSilver carburetor bolted to each cylinder head.

RIGHT The heart of the beast is this 120 cubic inch V-twin based on Harman cases, cylinders and heads. Each piston measures 4.325 inches across (a current Evo engine uses a 3.5 inch piston), flywheels are from S&S, camshaft is from Andrews.

FAR RIGHT How would you like to kick start 120 cubic inches of V-twin? Kick pedal connects to four-speed transmission, note the braided hose to the bottom of the transmission side cover indicating a hydraulic clutch-release mechanism. Unique exhaust pipes were fabricated by Neville.

are equipped with valves the size of pistons found in four-cylinder bikes and intake tracts designed to mount individual carburetors.

A QuickSilver 38mm slide carburetor feeds each of the giant cylinders while an Andrews B grind camshaft opens the intake and exhaust valves. A Crane ignition drives the coils, mounted up and out of the way under the gas tank. One-off upswept pipes, fabricated specially for this bike provide an exit route for the spent exhaust gases.

An open belt primary, this one measuring a full three inches across, takes the tractor torque of this monster motor to a four-speed transmission and Atlas clutch. A chain provides the final link between the engine and the 16-inch Dunlop rear tire. Both the belt primary and final chain drive are protected from debris and the rider's pants cuff by fabricated aluminum guards.

A 19-inch Dunlop mated to a dresser front fork assembly holds up the other end of this no-frills hauler. Both front and rear wheels mate aluminum rims with stainless spokes to create an assembly that's both good looking and strong. The same regard for quality is evident in the choice of brakes. In front, a pair of four-piston calipers from Performance Machine squeeze large-diameter floating front brake rotors while at the rear another PM four-piston caliper is paired to a smaller stainless steel rotor.

Though much of the equipment appears to be standard aftermarket components, most are fabricated or modified to fit. Neville fabricated the oil tank, for example, to include a box for the battery. The gas tank too received plenty of the customizer's attention. What seems to be a stock Sportster tank is actually an aftermarket "king" Sportster tank that Neville converted from dual gas fillers to a single flush-mount cap. The big Harman motor uses more than its fair share of external oil lines, all of them made from braided stainless hose with anodized aluminum fittings. The brakes are plumbed from master cylinder to caliper with similar high-grade braided components. Neville didn't intend to build a subtle motorcycle and the paint is nearly as loud as the bark from the fabricated exhaust pipes. The electric paint job by Tombstone in Castlemaine covers nearly everything, including the fenders, frame and engine drive pulley.

Like a lot of bike building projects this one started out as a simple rigid. That was before the Harman motor came along, followed by a long list of fabricated parts. What started as an inexpensive bar hopper turned into a rather exceptional rigid. What you might want to call a ravenous consumer of supposedly superior motorcycles.

ABOVE No two hardtails are alike. This example built by Neville Sharp of Melbourne, Australia uses a monster motor and high grade hardware to achieve a certain raw elegance.

HARDTAIL WITH A BOOST

OPPOSITE Externally the engine is extremely sanitary, which makes the turbo installation seem more like an integral part and less like a "bolt on" accessory. Many of the turbo controls are hidden under the gas tank. Engine uses three finishes to achieve the unusual look: grey powder coat, gloss black paint and standard chrome plate.

BELOW The unusual silhouette is created in part by the unique gas tank and front fender, combined with the bike's overall length.

To demonstrate that not all hardtails look the same or follow traditional lines, we present the unique and businesslike bike of Bob Frimpter from Five Bs in Waukesha, Wisconsin. Bob explains that he wanted a bike that was, "Narrow when you look at if from the rear. Like a thin line except for where the tank goes from narrow to wide. I used narrow glide trees and 39mm forks instead of a wide-glide fork to keep it thin."

The fattest thing on the whole bike might be the 180X18-inch Metzeler rear tire, mounted to a Akront rim laced to a Harley-Davidson hub with Buchanan spokes. At the front is a 19-inch Metzeler tire (not a 21) mounted to another high-quality rim, spoke and hub combination.

The front wheel is located by the 39mm fork legs, which use tubes that are actually one inch longer than stock. Each lower leg carries a four-piston Performance Machine caliper and each caliper squeezes a

slotted, polished rotor. The back uses four more four-piston calipers, all squeezing the same polished rotor.

Though the wheels and brakes might be top quality, it's between the wheels that this bike gets really interesting. Bob started with a set of Delkron cases, filled with 4-5/8 inches of S&S flywheel assembly. On top of that he added aluminum cylinders with a 3-1/2 inch bore from Harley-Davidson and heads from STD. The STD heads typically come in raw form so Bob did some porting work before installing new seats, Manley valves and 200-pound S&S valve springs.

What makes the stroker motor in Bob's hardtail interesting is the Aerocharger turbocharger, and the attention to detail that he used in assembling the engine.

To be absolutely sure he had enough power Bob set the boost level at 13 psi. That pressure is delivered to and through the Mikuni carburetor and eventually into the combustion chamber each time

ABOVE The more air you get in the cylinder (with more gas, of course) the more power the engine will make. Bob mounted the turbocharger to the left frame rail and adjusted the boost to 13 pounds. Intercooler is mounted ahead of the engine and is used to cool the pressurized air and thus make it more dense.

RIGHT Nineteen inch front rim is laced to the Harley-Davidson hub with twisted Buchanan spokes. Fabricated fender covers the Metzeler tire.

the recommended Aerocharger camshaft lifts an intake valve. In spite of the pressurized intake tract, the engine runs 9 to 1 static compression and burns pump premium gas. Detonation is not a problem, in part because the bike uses a Dyna ignition and two plugs per cylinder.

Externally this engine is just as interesting as it is internally. Instead of the standard polish and paint, Bob sent the cases and cylinders to Sumax for powder coating. Rather than use black or a color to match the bike, the crew at Sumax applied a grey powder doctored up with silver pearl flakes from House of Kolor. The color is subtle and has a flip-flop effect created by the pearl flakes. Anything that didn't get powder coated, like the outer primary and turbo housing, has been painted to match the rest of the bike.

Inside the primary housing is a Primo belt which takes the power to a five-speed transmission equipped with Andrews gears. Exiting the five-speed transmission is a standard final drive belt connected to the 70 tooth billet pulley.

Fat Bob tanks would hardly fit the long and skinny theme, so Bob cut up three tanks to create one long enough to fit the stretched Tripoli frame. The rear fender is a fiberglass fender supported by simple steel struts. The tech sheet lists the front fender as a Bob Frimpter special.

Mark Sporka from Menomonie Falls, Wisconsin, molded all the seams on the frame and sheet metal and applied the black paint, graphics and clearcoat. The color is actually a black pearl and changes with the angle and type of lighting - and of course the seat came from Danny Gray, seat-maker to the stars.

Bob set out to build a hardtail both slimmer and faster than all the rest. Not only that, it is more interesting, more complex and more like a drag bike than most other hardtails.

A SHOWCASE
HARDTAIL

Rob Carlson describes the small, flamed hardtail as a showcase bike. "We built the bike to showcase the abilities of our shop, and to give everybody on the crew a chance to participate in the project."

The shop in question is Kokesh MC, a small motorcycle shop located on Highway 65 just north of Minneapolis, Minnesota. At Kokesh they have very little staff turnover, most of the crew are both diehard motorcycle fanatics and long-term employees.

The concept started when Rob and his partner Gary Strom decided it might be fun to build a "shop bike." At the time it seemed everyone was building Softails, so they decided to build something different.

"We didn't realize," says Rob today, "that by the time we finished the bike everybody would be building hardtails."

Kokesh is what you might call a full-service shop. Not only do they sell parts for new and old Harley-Davidsons, they service those same bikes, restore old Knuckle and Panheads and build the occasional custom machine. Engine work is usually the domain of Lee Wickstrom and it was Lee who assembled the 80 cubic-inch V-twin starting with S&S engine cases and a flywheel assembly from Harley-Davidson. The aluminum cylinders, matching pistons and aluminum heads are all stock items.

The engine is far from being a stock item, however. Modifications include the special "Lee Wickstrom" cylinder heads. More than just a porting job, Lee welded up the stock ports before beginning the reshaping with the Dremel tool. Working in concert with the high-flow heads is a Viper cam from Mid-USA with .560 inches of lift and duration of 248 and 252 degrees for the intake and exhaust. Feeding the oversize intake tract is an oversize carburetor, the S&S Super G, normally seen on larger engines. The spark and ignition curve are provided by a Crane HI-4 ignition.

Behind the high-performance V-twin sits a high-performance five-speed transmission. Lee started with a Harley-Davidson case and added close-ratio gears from Andrews. Engine and transmission are connected by a standard primary chain.

While Lee worked on the engine, Elmer and "Bug" did the trial assembly, or mock-up, to ensure that all the parts would fit in both a mechanical and an aesthetic sense. Because they sell so many Atlas frames it was only natural to use an Atlas wide-drive chassis with three inches of stretch and a 38-degree fork angle. These wide-drive frames are designed to accept a fat rear tire, up to seven inches wide. Thus Elmer and Bug could install a 180X18 inch-Metzeler tire on an RC Components billet aluminum rim and still have room for belt drive. In front, another Metzeler tire, this one a 120X18-inch, was installed on another matching RC rim.

If you ask Rob why they chose these rims, his answer is simple, "We tried to use components we sell from companies we believe in. We like the RC rims because they fit, they're light in weight and they aren't too expensive."

Because it's such a light bike, a single front brake was deemed more than adequate. Bolted to the left lower leg is the Performance Machine four-piston, differential-bore caliper. For the rear wheel another Performance Machine caliper, this time a conventional four-piston design, squeezes another stainless-steel rotor.

Lee and Bug teamed up to build the front and rear fenders. Both started out as aftermarket steel fenders, modified and massaged into a more pleasing and unique shape. The rear fender in particular was strengthened so there would be no need for conventional fender struts. At the back of the fender is a nifty taillight that started life on an old Chevrolet before being adapted to fit the end of a motorcycle fender. Just ahead of the fender is another unique piece, the wrap-

around oil tank that comes back into a point on the left side to provide a place to mount the ignition switch.

An aftermarket gas tank was chosen, one with a pleasing shape that seemed to fit the frame and match the lines of the two fenders. Local upholstery wizard Mark Milbrant stitched up a special seat to Rob's specifications. "I wanted the seat to wrap down along the frame rails on either side," says Rob. "I did it that way to disguise the offset in the left side frame rail which is done to make room for the wide rear tire."

Once the bike came apart another local expert took over. Jerry Scherer applied the House of Kolor kosmos red urethane paint to the frame, fenders and most of the engine. And to make absolutely sure

their shop project received plenty of attention, Rob and Jerry decided on flames done with special one-off yellow paint mixed up by Jon Kosmoski from House of Kolor.

Before final assembly could begin, Jason ordered the rest of the parts needed to finish the red and yellow machine – the unusual White Brothers Exhaust pipe, Headwinds headlight and Krome Werks bars were all bolted in place.

The flamed hardtail succeeds as a showcase for Kokesh, not just because it's a very clean little bar hopper. The bike works because it's just a little different from all the other hardtails out there – much the way Kokesh itself is just a little different from all the other motorcycle shops up and down the street.

IT CAN BE SAID THAT 1981 WAS A SIGNIFICANT YEAR IN AMERICAN HISTORY. NOT BECAUSE A WAR BEGAN OR ENDED THAT YEAR OR BECAUSE OF SOME ENORMOUS POLITICAL SCANDAL. THE YEAR IS SIGNIFICANT BECAUSE ON JUNE 16, 1981 A GROUP OF HARLEY-DAVIDSON EXECUTIVES SIGNED THE PAPERS TO BUY THE COMPANY BACK FROM AMERICAN MACHINE AND FOUNDRY – MAKING HARLEY-DAVIDSON AN INDEPENDENT COMPANY ONCE AGAIN. THOUGH IT'S HARD TO BELIEVE TODAY, THE SUCCESS OF THE NEWLY INDEPENDENT VENTURE WAS ANYTHING BUT ASSURED. AMF BOUGHT THE MOTOR COMPANY IN 1969 AND DID MUCH TO INCREASE PRODUCTION OF HARLEY-DAVIDSON MOTORCYCLES. SOME WOULD SAY, HOWEVER, THAT THE INCREASED PRODUCTION CAME AT THE EXPENSE OF QUALITY.

RIGHT Most of the sheet metal on this sleek missile is from Harley-Davidson, including the front and rear fenders and the Fat Bob tanks. Orange paint is actually Tangelo pearl sprayed over a white basecoat to make it as bright as possible.

CUSTOM SOFTAIL

The Fat Bob tanks on this custom softail were stretched to match the long frame.

The radical swingarm on Andy Anderson's custom is based on the stock Harley-Davidson part. Modification includes the covers that hide the axle nuts and the chrome 'vents.' Rear caliper carries the signature milled pattern used throughout the bike.

At the front of this softail creation by Jon Dasheur is a factory style disc brake (you can only take the nostalgia thing so far), and a new spoked wheel with chrome rim and 16 inch Metzeler tire.

The early 1980s weren't a good time for large displacement motorcycles. Sales of the big bikes, a market segment that grew throughout the 1970s, began to drop in the early 1980s. Harley-Davidson was forced to compete for this shrinking market with an aging model lineup. Despite a loyal and hard core group of enthusiasts Harley-Davidson was hard pressed to sell enough motorcycles to keep the doors open.

In 1971 Harley-Davidson introduced the first Super Glide, which evolved into the Low Rider and eventually the Wide Glide. Despite the basic good looks of the Super Glides and Low Riders, they relied on the Shovelhead engine, four speed transmission and chain drive to the rear wheel. By the early 1980s these were dated machines (the Shovelhead engine first showed up in 1966) with a questionable reputation for quality.

Survival for Harley-Davidson meant the introduction of new models and updated drivetrains. In 1982 Harley-Davidson introduced a new line of bikes; the FXR models with rubber-mounted engines. The next big improvement came in 1984 with the unveiling of the Evolution engine. But there was another introduction in 1984 that played a bigger role in Harley's eventual success than any other.

Most industry insiders agree that the introduction of the Softail model in 1984 was the best marketing move ever made by Harley-Davidson. Based on a rear suspension design purchased from an individual customizer, the new chassis hid the rear shocks and springs under the frame. By using a triangulated swingarm the new Softail had the look of the earlier Hardtail frame without the harsh ride.

Before that time Harley-Davidson had the sound that everyone wanted, afterwards they had the sound *and* the look that defines an American motorcycle. Though the Softail chassis would eventually serve as the foundation for at least four families of machines, the first Softails made for a very popular factory custom.

Some call it the bike that saved Milwaukee. More than that, however, these factory customs seemed to beg for further modification by owners. When they introduced the Softail, Harley-Davidson assured their own survival, and also the survival of hundreds of small customizing and aftermarket shops.

Things haven't changes all that much in the ensuing years. Softails are still the most popular bikes built by Harley-Davidson and they still beg for further refinement by the owners. Go to Daytona or Sturgis, or any Harley-Davidson event, and you find Softails by the hundreds and thousands, customized in every possible color and style.

The bikes seen here represent an overview of the multitude of Softails customized, painted and rebuilt in garages all over the world. Some owners reach backward with early sheet metal and springer forks to create a new bike that looks genuinely old, while others install the latest billet aluminum wheels and accessories, and apply the brightest neon colors imaginable. Whether new or old they all have a few things in common: they're all bright, bold and beautiful.

A MODERN SEAMLESS SOFTAIL

ABOVE The Wizard seen on the dash is more of the airbrush work from the talented Mr. Stevens.

CENTER Shaun Christian's orange Softail gets much of its sleek appearance from the stretched Pro One frame and the 38 degree fork angle.

Shaun Christian is a man deeply involved with vehicles, both the two and four-wheeled variety. Though he's best known as the creator of sophisticated show vehicles for stereo component companies like Kicker, Shaun has been building equally loud two wheeled vehicles for a number of years now. His orange Softail might be called the evolutionary end of a series.

"When I built this bike," explains Shaun, "I knew exactly how I wanted it to look. We'd built two earlier Softail bikes and I liked their lines, for this one I wanted to go with the same basic idea but take it farther. I wanted this bike to be smoother and more finished."

The smoothness of the machine starts dead center with the special one-piece Fat Bob tanks and integral dash. Bob at Carefree Highway Truckin' in Tulsa, Oklahoma is the man responsible for all the nice metal and molding work. Bob started with separate five gallon Fat Bob tanks and a dash from Pro One. By the time he was done the two tanks and single dash were magically merged into one seamless piece.

The transformation started with a new extended tail for each tank. Because the two tanks were to be made one, Bob had to design a new

"drop on" mounting system in place of the standard side mounts used on late model Fat Bob tanks. After welding the two tanks into one unit Bob welded on the metal dash from Pro One.

Shaun likes to use factory sheet metal whenever possible because, as he says, "It's metal, it's good quality, and it's a good value for the price." Thus Carefree Bob created the rear fender by first widening a Fat Boy rear fender and then welding that to a pair of Pro One fender struts. Before he was finished, Bob added a flush-mount LED tail and brake light and a nifty slide-in-from-behind license plate mounting system. Unlike the rear fender, the Fat Boy front fender was left in "as stamped" condition and prepped for paint.

Shaun wanted his hot rod really sm-o-o-o-o-th, so everything on the bike was molded including all fabrication work, as well as the welds on the Pro One frame. The orange paint is actually a tangelo pearl hue from the House of Kolor sprayed over a white base. When Bob finished with the paint Cole Stevens added airbrush graphics before turning the parts over to "The Wizard" for final pinstriping.

The V-twin in Shaun's orange crush measures 80 cubic inches and

was designed to be "a dependable, fun, street motor." Shaun goes on to explain that this bike was built to be his regular ride. "We started with a complete 80 cubic inch motor from Harley-Davidson, and left most of it stock. Donny Meador at Kinetic Playground in Tulsa did all the work. He only changed the cam, pushrods, carb, ignition and the pipes."

In place of those stock components Donny used a Head Quarters camshaft and pushrods, a Super E carburetor from S&S, a Dyna S ignition and pipes from Vance & Hines. If Shaun took a conservative bent internally, he did the just the opposite with the engine's externals. This motor is so bright it's hard to look at on a sunny day. The cases are polished while the cylinders are polished, de-finned and then painted orange to match the bike. Chrome plated rocker boxes top it all off, complimented by a plated primary cover, billet derby and inspection covers and an Arlen Ness cam cover.

Even the transmission case was polished before being filled with Andrews gears and a roller bearing trap door. A BDL belt-drive primary connects engine and transmission, while a stock belt is used between the transmission and rear wheel.

The final-drive belt mates to a RC Components 70 tooth rear sprocket, which in turn bolts to a RC 18X5.5 inch billet wheel equipped with an Avon 180 series tire. A matching 18 inch wheel, this one equipped with a 3.5 inch rim, mounts between the 39mm wide glide fork legs. Polished PM four-piston calipers, one on each end, squeeze ventilated rotors to slow everything down.

When all the outside craftsmen were finished Shaun and crew assembled the engine and transmission, fenders, wheels, calipers and rotors into a complete motorcycle. As part of the final assembly, to improve the overall look of the bike, Shaun hid all the wiring inside the frame and moved the ignition switch to a small housing just behind the rear cylinder. Final hardware choices include a Headwinds headlight, billet forward controls from PM and grips from Arlen Ness. The neatly fitting solo seat is the handwork of Southeast Auto Trim in Tulsa.

The end result of all the careful planning, fabrication and assembly is a very professional and finished motorcycle. What you might call Shaun's seamless Softail.

ABOVE The ignition switch on this seamless beauty has been moved to the pod below the seat and routed all the wiring inside the frame. Engine cases, cylinder and heads have all been polished. Cylinders and heads were then painted orange, between the fins, to match the rest of the bike.

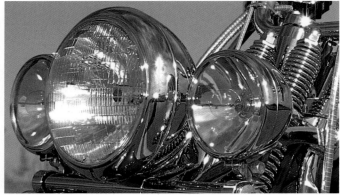

NEW PARTS MAKE AN OLD MOTORCYCLE

ABOVE To create a true Hardtail impression, Jon Dasheur used a rear fender with no external struts. Beehive taillight, rear support stand and early-style luggage rack all work to create the look of a 1936 Harley VL.

ABOVE RIGHT The large diameter headlight and twin spot lights all mount to a fabricated light bar. Bullet shaped clearance lights are used as turn signals.

OPPOSITE The engine in Jon's machine is an 80-cubic-inch Evo built with a combination of aftermarket and Harley-Davidson parts. Early style oil filter, horn and exhaust work in harmony with the styling cues used throughout the bike.

When Jon Dasheur from Faribault, Minnesota decided to take a bold step and build his own motorcycle, he resisted the temptation to run out and start buying parts. Instead, Jon took the time to plan exactly what the bike should look like. The idea was to build a "springer," but not the typical chopper-style of springer with a long fork and 21 inch front wheel.

"What I really wanted was a new bike with the look of a 1936 Harley VL," explains Jon. "The first big problem was finding a front fork, because at that time Harley didn't make a springer designed to run a 16 inch wheel. So I bought a two-inch-under fork from Sundance and an early style front fender from V-Twin."

Mating the V-Twin fender to the Sundance fork proved a difficult task for at least two reasons. First, Jon had to narrow the fender to make it fit between the legs of the fork. Second, he had to design linkage that would keep the fender the same distance from the tire as the tire went up and down over bumps.

Paul Chergosky from Anoka, Minnesota is the man responsible for the modified fork. He's also the man who designed and installed the support assembly up inside the Softail rear fender and figured out how to mount it to the frame with four bolts hidden under the seat. The whole idea of course was to make this look like a more convincing hardtail from 1936. The stubby fork and strut-less rear fender bolt to a Paughco Softail-style frame. Because the goal was a retro bike, Jon ordered the frame without any additional rake or stretch. Up front, Jon and his wife Susan fabricated the light bar and brackets that mount the headlight and spotlights. In back, an early-style five-bar luggage rack was purchased, then narrowed to hold only four bars and better fit the proportions of the bike. To accommodate an occasional passenger Jon found a pillion pad from Corbin that bolts to the same four holes used to mount the luggage rack.

Even though the machine that first fired Jon's imagination gleamed in red, Tracy at TJ Design in Shakopee, Minnesota molded the frame and sheet metal and then painted the bike and frame in vibrant blue. Both the front and rear fenders were then edged in silver and gold leaf. The tanks received the same treatment, a combination of silver leaf in the shape of an eagle's claw, with a diamond shaped gold leaf inset, pinstriped and lettered by hand. Multiple clearcoats bury the ultra thin strips of metal and pinstriping so the paint surface is both seamless and ultra glossy.

The power for Jon's retro springer comes from a 80 cubic inch Evo style engine based on STD cases combined with Harley-Davidson cylinders and heads. The relatively mild V-twin uses a Keihin CV-style carburetor equipped with a Harley-Davidson air cleaner and two-into one exhaust complete with a fishtail tip. The cylinders are painted blue to match the bike while the heads are painted silver. Primary, cam and derby covers are all made-in-Milwaukee items. The derby and inspection covers carry the Harley logo in gold so it matches the air cleaner and works in harmony with the gold leaf used on the fenders and tank.

American Thunder in Shakopee, Minnesota helped Jon with the final assembly of the bike. Neal and the crew installed the engine and stock five speed transmission, and connected the two with a BDL primary-belt. Another belt, this one from Harley-Davidson, carries the power from the transmission to the sixteen inch rear wheel. Forward controls for the five speed tranny and the Harley-Davidson rear disc brake are from JayBrake.

Jon wanted floor boards up front, in addition to the highway pegs. At back he chose a beehive taillight flanked on either side by simple early-style marker lights, used in this case as blinkers. Below the fender lip hangs the old-style stand; like many of the parts on this bike the stand had to be modified to fit and then sent out to Brown's for chrome plating. Final assembly details include the chrome wrap used on all the cables, the invisible wiring, and the early style horn and oil filter.

More than money, this project required time: time to find the right parts, the right artists and the right mechanics who could transform a certain new/old motorcycle from fantasy to reality.

A TWO-WHEELED **CANVAS**

Ask Andy Anderson from Nashville, Tennessee how he conceived the ultra bright Softail, and he explains that the idea to was create more than just a custom motorcycle.

"I didn't want a frame with a front fender, tanks and a rear fender," he explains. "The goal was a bike that would be one integral unit, one whole piece of mechanical art. Each part of the puzzle needed to blend with the others instead of standing alone."

The sheet metal Andy worked so hard to design and fabricate bolts to the remains of a 1995 Harley-Davidson Softail chassis. Though some people work with aftermarket frames, Andy describes himself as a traditionalist: "the Harley-Davidson title means a lot to me," he explains. The modified frame is nearly three inches longer than a stocker, and mounts the fork at a longish thirty-eight degree angle.

The 41mm wide glide fork assembly from the original bike is now mated to Dresser lower legs with caliper mounting lugs on either side. The four-piston calipers are from PM and each one carries the special milled pattern that Andy used throughout the bike. Andy and his

friend José designed the trick one-off billet aluminum triple trees, carved on CNC equipment at Thunder Heart in Andy's home town of Nashville. The triple trees feature a stepped design and internal hydraulic circuits so the brake lines actually thread into the lower triple tree instead of a conventional T. Between the two fork legs is a 21 inch billet wheel from Arlen Ness, rotating on a flush-mount Donnie-Smith axle.

Milwaukee Iron did the rough sheet metal fabrication, per Andy's renderings. The finish work, however, is Andy's own, thus the tanks fit very precisely to the neck area and the dash itself fits with such precision that the two tanks merge and become one. The rear fender and side covers are good examples of the collaboration between Andy and Randy from Milwaukee Iron. The raw fender with its internal support was crafted by Randy, though Andy fabricated the taillight housing and the curved taillight lens. The design includes a seat that is Frenched into the fender and repeats the graphic design seen in the paint. Andy sent the seat pan and detailed sketches to Danny Gray,

who earned his undying respect for crafting what Andy calls an "absolutely perfect seat." Like all the panels on this bike, the side covers blend right into the rear fender, though they are in fact separate pieces.

The swingarm is another piece of fine art. Crafted from the original, the triangular design uses covers, painted to match the bike, to hide the axle nuts, with small stainless "vents" at the front of the design. In order to run the wide, 160X17 inch tire, Andy used a relatively narrow billet pulley and drive belt designed for a Sportster.

Painted in a blend of candy magenta and hot pink, the engine for Andy's artistic two wheeler measures 89 cubic inches. External refinements include the polished factory cases, and cylinders with a special milled pattern that runs diagonally across each cylinder, the work of John Bryant in Cleveland, Ohio. Derby, inspection and transmission covers all come from the Florida shop of Clyde McCullough and each carries the milled signature of Andy Anderson.

The extra cubes were obtained with a stroker, 4-5/8 inch flywheel assembly from S&S, mated to cylinders with stock internal dimensions. The Harley heads were converted to dual plug status and encouraged to flow more air with help from Red Rhea at R&B Cycles in Nashville. A pair of Quicksilver carbs mounted behind a billet air cleaner feed gas and air to the stroker motor each time the Crane cam opens one of Red's massaged intake valves. Exhaust valves dump into a pair of very unique pipes - the best excuse to buy a TIG welder.

"First I drew up about 15 different designs on paper until I had something that seemed to fit the bike," explains Andy. "Then I bought a lot of raw 1-3/4 inch pipe, curves in various shapes and some straight sections, from a local supplier and stitched them together."

In order to paint the bike, Andy assembled the complete machine, minus the engine, sprayed the whole thing with yellow base coat mixed from House of Kolor Shimrins, and then proceeded to do a very complex layout with thin fine line tape. Next, all the graphic areas received a silver basecoat before application of the House of Kolor kandies could begin. Andy created each spear and oval in multiple stages, blending various mixes of kandies so each one contains subtle color changes and shadings. One look at the machine and it's not hard to believe Andy spent nearly a month on the paint job alone.

That same fanaticism was used in the handle bars. The set on the bike is the sixth set that Andy made, but the first to meet his high standards - including invisible wiring, integral speedometer housing and nearly invisible switches used for turn signals.

Though he seems unable to build a mild custom, Andy Anderson certainly succeeds when it comes to creating something more - a very unique piece of two-wheeled mechanical art.

ABOVE Andy Anderson spent considerable time doing sketches and colored renderings before he decided on one design he really liked. The goal was a machine where each fender or exhaust pipe became a blended portion of the overall machine and not an individual part.

LEFT Elaborate paint job required that each spear and arch be masked off separately. Then Andy would apply the basecoat followed by multiple coats of a special-mix candy color. After drying that spear could be masked over and Andy would start on another area.

IT WAS SUPPOSED TO BE EASY

Tom Rose from Minneapolis, Minnesota, already owned a perfectly good motorcycle. A Harley-Davidson Softail with trick paint and nice wheels. But then everyone else started to show up with bikes smarter than Tom's. Specifically, these new customs had the really fat rear tire, the 200 series monster from Avon.

To rectify this deficiency in the tire department, Tom took his Softail to Mike McAllister at M-C Specialties in Blaine, Minnesota. Together they worked out a plan to install a new swingarm and new wheels. The new rear wheel would of course carry the object of Tom's lust, a 200X16 gumball from Avon.

The ultra-wide rear tire required a new rear fender, and it was during this discussion of fenders that the project began to get out of hand. Instead of mounting a catalog fender with the standard fender struts Mike suggested that he could create a trick fender with internal struts. Tom readily agreed and that might have been the end of the matter, except for one thing.

Tom asked Mike if they could add more rake to the front of the bike, at which time Mike suggested that they create a whole new front frame section with better aesthetics and additional stretch, instead of just adding to the rake. Again, Tom agreed, so Mike and his merry crew went to work building a new rear fender and a complete front frame section.

Installing the new swingarm meant disassembly of the primary drive on the bike's left side. Once the primary drive and most of the sheet metal was removed, Mike called Tom to report he was, "about two bolts short of having the motor out of the frame."

Pulling the motor out of the frame would open up a whole raft of creative possibilities. Up to this point Mike and Tom planned to paint the new frame section black to match the existing frame, and then simply paint the new rear fender to match the rest of the sheet metal.

Of course it turned out Tom already had a flashy paint job in mind. Mike's phone call provided the excuse he needed, a means to justify the added expense of the complete repaint. Once they decided on a bright paint job by local craftsman Bruce Bush, there was, in Mike's words, "no turning back."

The new attitude meant that Mike could fabricate a set of handle bars designed specifically to fit Tom, from stainless-steel tubing. Like the bars, the seat is a one-off crafted by Kevin Lehan. Because the rear fender has no provision for a taillight, Mike used a side-mount license plate bracket and light assembly.

Though they elected to leave the already modified engine alone, a new coil bracket and covers were added to the left side. The bracket also contains the ignition and start switch which took all the switches off the handle bars. The simplified wiring meant a simplified harness, one that Mike could hide inside the frame before beginning the reassembly.

RIGHT Whether they're two-wheelers or four-wheelers all true hot rods have fat tires. This 200 series Avon mounts to a 6-inch wide rim so it's just a little wider than the same tire on a 5-inch rim.

OPPOSITE The engine in Tom's new Softail is a "hot rod 80" - a motor with increased power obtained through the use of a performance carburetor, camshaft, pipes and ignition, and no change in displacement.

FAR LEFT Left side shows the stretched tanks with trim dash. Cylinders and heads have been polished and painted. Chrome primary cover and billet floorboards add more shine to this already bright machine.

LEFT Coils are mounted on a billet aluminum bracket hung on the engine's left side, per current custom practice. Yellow plug wires add a nice touch.

As the bike came back together there were a few more snags. The 200 series tire mounted on a six-inch Performance Machine rim did fit, but left no room for the existing brakes. The answer: new brakes from Performance Machine. With everything gleaming and new, the old exhaust system just wouldn't do so Mike installed a new pipe and muffler combination from Vance & Hines. Most of the plated or polished parts went to either Brown's Plating in Texas or Deter's Polishing in nearby Fridley.

Like a snowball tumbling downhill, Tom and Mike's project picked up speed and momentum as it rolled. The project that both thought would be easy to do and relatively inexpensive to complete turned out to be neither easy nor cheap. Tom, however, is philosophical - "You get what you pay for. This is not the bike I ordered - this is the bike I really wanted."

LEFT Mike and Tom used a 19-inch front tire from Avon, mounted to a PM wheel and slowed by a single PM caliper. The new front frame section includes the front downtubes, which are larger diameter than stock for a beefier look.

MORE CHALLENGING
THAN MOST

Sputhe rocker boxes top off the polished and painted cylinders and heads. Cam cover and transmission right side cover carry a Donnie Smith design. Fat tanks and Street Sweeper air cleaner cover show off the graphic talents of Lenni Schwartz.

Well-known bike builder Donnie Smith considers each new project to be a challenge. Some, however, are more challenging than others. When Chrome Specialties asked him to build a bike based on a number of their new products, Donnie didn't think the job would be too tough. Not, that is, until they specified which parts he had to use and what kind of a look they wanted the bike to have.

"They wanted to use the new seven-gallon Fat Bob tanks," explains Donnie, "and the inverted fork with a big 150-by-16-inch front tire. Usually we build Harleys to be pretty narrow, now they wanted me to build a bike that was fat, almost bulky."

Not surprisingly, most of the parts on this bike come from the Chrome Specialties (often abbreviated, CSI) catalog. The Jammer Softail-style frame arrived at Donnie's shop with no stretch and a modest rake angle. Donnie of course immediately did what he calls a "wedge rake" to increase the fork angle to about 37 degrees. The fork

itself is an inverted design, said to be stronger because these assemblies mount the larger diameter part of the fork in the triple trees so there is less flexing during braking and cornering.

Donnie explains that while the forks might be great, the triple trees that came with the forks left much to be desired. "We built our own triple trees from aluminum because the trees that came with the forks looked pretty chunky with big pinch bolts sticking out. We made a pair of trees with hidden bolts and the split in the backside where you can't see it. We also took the forks apart and changed the springs to lower the front end of the bike about two inches."

At the other end of the bike Donnie and crew installed the X-Drive swingarm, one of the new products that Donnie designed for CSI. The X-Drive makes it possible to install a 200X16-inch tire in a standard Softail frame.

Key to the whole project was the use of the new, extra large, seven-gallon Fat Bob gas tanks. Rob Roehl, Donnie's sheet metal man, formed sheet metal tails for the end of each tank. With the extensions in place the tanks wrap around the front edge of the seat and extend back to neatly meet the frame rails. Of course the longer tanks needed a longer dash, accomplished by extending the Jammer dash

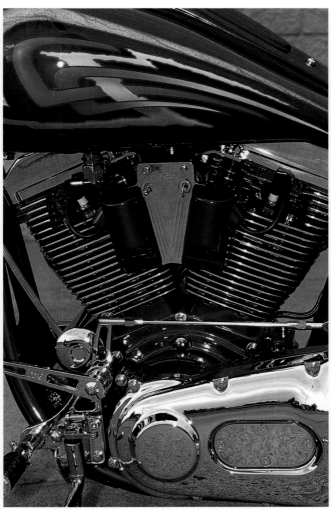

to come back all the way to the edge of the custom Keith Nybo seat.

The purple bike turned out to be more than just an exercise in bike building. Many of the parts designed for this bike have since gone into production and are now catalog items. The rear fender struts, for example, are part of the Donnie Smith Design Signature Series offered for sale by CSI. The fenders themselves come from the West Coast shop of Jesse James.

To power the new rotund motorcycle Donnie ordered a 96-cubic-inch engine complete from S&S. Instead of buying the motor already assembled, Donnie bought it in parts, so the fins on the cylinders and heads could be polished, before the cases, cylinders and heads were painted in purple to match everything else. Don Tima, Donnie's engine man, then carefully assembled all the new parts into a complete V-twin.

The complete five-speed transmission, primary chain and final belt drive all came from the CSI catalog. Before installation, the transmission case received a coat of that same purple paint, a chrome top cover and a new Donnie Smith side cover.

The trend in spoked wheels is to more spokes, so Donnie chose 80-spoke wheels from Hallcraft, a 16X3½-inch in front and a 16X5 inch in the back. Three floating rotors, two in front and one at the back,

matched to four-piston Motor Factory brake calipers provide premium braking power for the big, purple Packard.

Another interesting innovation is the handle bars. Unlike most bars, these are made from 1-½ inch tubing, so the bars are the same size as the mounts for the master cylinder and the CSI grips. The big bars look so clean that one wonders why nobody did this before.

This massive bike gets its look from the larger-than-life sheet metal, the fat tires used on both ends, and the passion purple House of Kolor paint applied by Brian Mahler with graphics by Lenni Schwartz.

If Donnie had doubts about the bike when he started, those doubts were quickly erased by the time the bike rolled out of the shop for the first time. "When we started on the bike the guys in the shop didn't want to work on it," says Donnie with a smile. "But when it started to come together, all of a sudden everybody wanted to work on the purple bike and was hanging around that hoist."

The crew proved a good barometer of public reaction, Moby Grape draws a crowd wherever it is parked. What started out as a "challenging" project turned out to be a huge success for both Donnie Smith and CSI.

ABOVE Fat is where it's at. Donnie's crew stretched the tanks to wrap around the front of the seat and then stretched the dash to match. Note the large-diameter bars and the billet speedometer cover.

ABOVE LEFT Until recently the inverted fork designs were seen only on competition or sport bikes. This 34mm design from CSI fits most current Harley-Davidsons. The "upside-down" forks give riders a stronger assembly and a new look for the front of the bike.

ABOVE CENTER On the left side is the Donnie Smith billet coil bracket, with ignition switch and painted coil covers. Forward controls are from AMS.

A HOME-RUN HIT

If Donnie Smith's purple bike is a bit on the heavy side, then the orange machine is at the other end of the scale. Like a young athlete, this orange Softail is trim and taut, unable to relax, always ready to compete. And like an athlete, each part of the machine contributes to the overall sense of perfection.

At the front this bike rides on a slim 19 inch Avon tire mounted on a Performance Machine wheel. The narrow-glide fork is a Donnie Smith original, made up by installing 41mm fork tubes in fabricated aluminum triple trees. Twin six-piston calipers from Performance Machine are mounted on the Pro One lower legs on either side, with rotors from PM designed to match the wheels.

The front wheel with its skinny hot rod fender seems to reach out ahead of the bike, placed there by the 38-degree fork angle. There is no air dam between the front wheel and the frame, instead this bike carries a belly pan that gives a much more finished look to the Daytec frame.

The long, slim gas tank is a perfect fit for the rest of the bike. If you ask Donnie how he achieved such a nice shape for the tank, he gives all the credit to his metal man, "We started with an aftermarket tank, a Mustang tank," explains Donnie. "I just gave the tank to Rob and he did his magic. Part of what makes it such a nice shape is the raised section along the top, it gives the tank some character and makes it seem longer."

Behind the tank is a one-off solo seat built by Keith Nybo and behind that is the minimalist fender with internal struts, more of Rob's handiwork. While some oil tanks just sit there, this one fits snugly into the curve of the frame, the gap between the tank and frame exactly the same all along the top and the back side.

Contributing to the long lean look of this bike are the hand-fabricated exhaust pipes. The two pipes run side by side, fairly high up on the bike. Each is marred by only a small bulge indicating that there might be some baffles in there after all. The pipes are slash cut at the end, with the angle of the slash a perfect match to the angle of the swingarm.

An athlete needs to be able to run and run hard. With 113 cubic inches of V-twin heart, there aren't many street machines that this bike can't outrun. Based on the new 4-inch-bore S&S cases and cylinders, this particular combination uses a 4-1/2 inch flywheel assembly to achieve the massive displacement figure. Purchased in pieces, the cylinders and heads were polished and then painted orange, like the engine cases and even the transmission.

Don Tima, engine man for Donnie Smith, carefully balanced the flywheels before proceeding with the rest of the engine assembly. Internally, this engine has all brand new S&S components, each chosen for fit and maximum mechanical harmony. Externally the engine shines with paint, polish or chrome, the parts chosen for simplicity and visual impact. Look closely, and you will see that even the grade 8 chrome Allen bolts have small chrome caps.

All that horsepower needs a good connection to the ground. The 200X16 Avon rear tire mounted on another Performance Machine wheel might be called the "Air-Nike" of motorcycle tires. On the left side of the five-spoke wheel is one of the mechanical features that

helps to put this bike in a class by itself. The very compact brake caliper sits in the apex of the swingarm where it almost disappears. If the motorcycle aftermarket gave awards for "Best Engineered New Product," this rear brake would be sure to take top honors. Not only is the caliper mounting unobtrusive, the rotor is bolted to the inside of the rear brake pulley and the brake line runs inside the swingarm. The whole package, developed jointly by Donnie and Leo DiOrio, is extremely trim, compact and well engineered.

Donnie built the bike for James Shapiro, who chose the color after seeing an orange Panhead in the shop before construction started on his own bike. The color is actually tangelo from the House of Kolor, applied by Brain Mahler. The seamless frame is the result of Greg Smith's careful molding, and the unusual "tribal flames" are by Lenni Schwartz.

Perfection is a difficult thing to achieve. For an athlete it comes after endless training. For a certain tangelo motorcycle, the person doing the training is the builder, who after over 20 years of building custom motorcycles just hit another home run over the fence and out onto the street.

OPPOSITE Braided "oil" line leading up to the right side transmission case means this is a hydraulic, not cable-actuated, clutch. The motor on modern customs does more than power the machine - the good ones also contribute to the overall visual package. Note the polished and painted cylinders and heads, the painted engine and transmission cases, the phenomenal attention to detail.

BELOW Gas tank is a perfect fit for the bike, both in a visual and a literal sense. Unique graphics by Lenni Schwartz are a hybrid mix of tribal design and traditional flames.

RIGHT If you look very closely you see the brake caliper mounted in the center of the swingarm, and the rotor mounted to the rim of the rear wheel pulley. The brake line runs inside the tubing for the rear swingarm.

DARE TO BE DIFFERENT

Most custom machines are created as part of a carefully orchestrated plan. Yet, as Dave Perewitz explains, there are some that seem to happen almost by accident. "I took this Springer Softail in on trade for another bike," explains Dave. "It was so beat up that I had to do something. We started to patch the thing up for a quick sale, but one thing led to another and all of a sudden we were building a complete custom. Once I realized the project was out of hand we decided to go all the way and build a full custom."

Full custom for Dave Perewitz means a longer bike with the front wheel pushed out ahead of the frame. To meet these parameters Dave's small crew cut off the front of the frame and built a new tubular extension. The net result is a frame three inches longer than stock with a fork angle of 36 degrees.

What sets this bike apart from other Dave Perewitz bikes are the long fenders. These were a departure for Dave, who normally runs rather abbreviated fenders on both the front and rear. "We decided to do something different with this bike," says Dave. "I decided to take a risk and try these new, long fenders from Jesse James. The length and the way we cut off the rear fender gives the bike a unique look."

The missing ignition switch can be found on the left side, between the coils in the Perewitz billet coil bracket. By eliminating the turn signals David was able to eliminate any switches on the Arlen Ness handle bars.

When the time came to do something with the engine it didn't make much sense to install a mild 80-cubic-inch engine in the stretched frame with the smart sheet metal. After breaking the engine down to the bare cases all the external pieces went to Rhode Island Tech for polishing. Next, the cylinders and heads were carefully masked off so the areas between the fins could be painted blue to match the rest of the bike.

Al Wenkus from Waltham, Massachusetts, is the man who gathered up all the polished and painted pieces and assembled them into a running whole. Al used a 4-$\frac{5}{8}$ inch stroker flywheel assembly coupled with 3-$\frac{1}{2}$ inch pistons, both from S&S, to create an 89 cubic inch V-twin. On top of the cylinders are the Harley-Davidson heads equipped with new valves and a porting job by Boston-area expert Jim Thompson.

A Crane camshaft opens the intake and exhaust valves, allowing the stroker to inhale through a Mikuni carburetor and exhale into a set of Bub exhaust pipes. Perewitz billet rocker boxes top off the heads, while Arlen Ness cam and primary covers add more sparkle to either side of the V-twin.

Fast motorcycles need effective brakes and Dave chose a single GMA four-piston brake caliper at the front squeezing a polished rotor designed to match the wheels. When it came time to choose a fork, Dave picked one of his own super-smooth Wide-Glide assemblies. At the back the just-blue bike uses Progressive shocks designed to lower the rear by about one inch. The rear brakes mimic those on the front with another GMA caliper and another rotor designed to match the wheels. On the left side is another shiny piece of aluminum intended to match the design of the wheels, the 70-tooth belt pulley.

Before final assembly, Russ and Don at Cycle Fab molded the frame and all the sheet metal components to eliminate any seams and prepped the parts for paint. The true-blue paint is a pearl hue from House of Kolor, applied by Russ and David in the Cycle Fab paint booth. And in keeping with the bike's dare-to-be-different theme, David chose to delete the standard graphics package and leave the bike in straight blue.

So what you have is a typically sanitary Perewitz custom with a twist. A true-blue beauty with new-wave fenders and no graphics.

LEFT Too blue Softail uses no graphics, just blue urethane for the stretched tanks, fenders, air cleaner and even the rear fender struts. A big fan of the ultra sanitary look, Perewitz bikes use no gauges on the bars and just a simple smooth non-dash between the tanks. Note the air cleaner cover designed to mimic the shape of the tank, as well as the Perewitz/Sullivan fork assembly and billet wheels.

BELOW Sleek fender struts mount the fender low over the rear tire. GMA caliper is mounted directly below the axle, instead of in the apex of the swingarm. The swingarm itself had to be modified so David's crew could mount the 180X18-inch rear tire.

Underneath the long fenders are two 18-inch Avon tires mounted on Perewitz/Sullivan billet wheels. The sidewalls read 130/80X18 in front and 180/55X18 in back. In order to mount the wide 18-inch tire the boys at Cycle Fab re-engineered the stock swingarm to make room for both the fat-attack tire and the factory belt drive.

The long stretched gas tanks are more typical of a Dave Perewitz custom. Jed, metal man at Cycle Fab, started with five-gallon Fat Bob tanks and added "tails" that stretch the tanks to fit the longer frame and wrap around the front of the Danny Gray seat. Between the tanks is the typical Perewitz understated dash with no speedometer, no tach, no warning lights and no ignition switch.

A SHOVELHEADED SOFTAIL

In a very short space of time, the venerable Shovelhead engine has developed from current powerplant to "nearly antique" status. Evolution engines, introduced in 1984, have become so dominant that no one even thinks about building a "custom" bike with a Shovelhead engine.

Of course there are exceptions to every rule. When Jesse Keen from Harrisburg, Pennsylvania, decided he needed a custom Harley, it never occurred to him to cut up a new Softail with an Evolution engine. He already owned a nice old Wide Glide and it seemed the logical place to start. For help Jesse called longtime friend and bike builder Ed Kerr.

Ed and Jesse put together a plan to transform the old Shovelhead into something longer, brighter and much more modern - yet still powered by the Shovelhead engine. Though some builders would have opened a catalog and ordered up a new frame from Arlen Ness or Kenny Boyce, Jesse and Ed elected to stay with the old FX frame from The Motor Company. Ed thought that with a little imagination and a lot of fabrication he could transform the old frame into a more modern foundation for a new bike.

The fabrication Ed had in mind went beyond the standard stretch and rake treatment. If Softails are all the rage, why not discard the old shocks and their mounts and position the new shocks under the bike?

Ed "borrowed" the suspension geometry from a standard Softail, but he still had to determine where on the frame to locate the mount for the shocks. For a swingarm Ed elected to keep the stock piece, with a new fabricated mount for the shocks. The actual fabrication and welding is the work of Randy Wolfe from Mechanicsburg, Pennsylvania. Randy, who spends most of his time fabricating race car frames, also created a new front frame section which stretches the bike five inches and helps to give it those nice lines.

Hanging on the long, stretched frame is a pair of long, stretched gas tanks. Ed added extra metal at the back of the tanks, mounted them low and gave the bottom of the tanks a concave shape. For fenders he used Tail Draggers from the Arlen Ness catalog, a thin one in front and a standard eight-inch wide model in the rear. Rather than mount the taillight on the fender, Ed chose to build a small bracket, supported by tubular aluminum, to hold both the taillight and the license plate bracket. As part of the smooth and modern treatment, Ed and Jesse decided that the battery had to move from its stock external location to the center of the wrap-around oil tank.

The Wide Glide forks are supported by polished Billet Concept triple trees and the lower legs are brand new units from Custom Chrome. The twin four-piston calipers used at the front carry the familiar PM logo as does the matching caliper used in the back. Spoked wheels,

FAR RIGHT The billet air cleaner, chrome plated rocker boxes, polished cylinders and heads, all make the old Shovelhead sparkle. The early style engine helps give this bike a classic flavor.

BELOW RIGHT The Arlen Ness front fender wraps around a 21-inch spoked rim. Twin Performance Machine calipers squeeze ventilated rotors.

BELOW Though it has been molded and extended, the frame underneath that gorgeous sheet metal is pure Harley-Davidson. The long frame, Arlen Ness fenders and stretched tanks give the bike a very modern flavor.

measuring 21 inches in front and 16 in the rear, help the bike retain a classic flavor.

Mike Magaro from Harrisburg did a complete overhaul on the Shovelhead. The rebuild included the installation of a new stroker flywheel assembly from S&S and an Andrews 485 B-grind cam. They say that Shovelheads don't breathe as well as the newer Evos, but after Mike finished the porting work, Jesse's heads flow considerably more air than they did before. In order to ensure that those enlarged ports get enough air and fuel, Mike used a new S&S Shorty carburetor hidden under a billet air cleaner from Arlen Ness.

Externally, the engine and four-speed transmission are as bright as Librandis Plating in Middletown, Pennsylvania, could make them. The cylinders are minus the bottom fins and polished to a high luster. The heads suffer from an overdose of tripoli polishing compound and the rocker boxes are chrome-plated. Both the engine and transmission cases are fully polished and all the covers, brackets and levers are either polished or plated.

Before final assembly could begin, Ed and Jesse packed up all the frame and sheet metal parts and shipped them down to Brockton, Massachusetts, home of Cycle Fab. Dave Perewitz and his brother Donnie molded the frame, smoothed the sheet metal seams and then applied the Porsche cobalt blue from the House of Kolor. Roy Mason and Nancy Brooks did the graphics, before the brothers Perewitz applied the final clearcoats.

Final assembly took place in Ed's small shop just in time to pack the bike up and ship it off for the first trip to Sturgis. Since that outing Ed and Jesse have seen plenty of beautiful custom bikes. Fancy lowered dressers, long rakish FXRs and more Softails than they could count. But among all those hundreds of thousands of motorcycles, they've only seen one Shovel-powered fabricated Softail.

A ROWDY CUSTOM

Jeff Beebe describes his latest custom V-twin as "rowdy." "I don't like to ride the same machines as everyone else," explains Jeff. "If you look in the parking lot, there are plenty of bikes with a three-inch stretch and 34 degrees of rake. So I figured I'd go all the way. This frame has five inches of stretch and a fork angle of 38 degrees, it looks like a freight train."

The uniqueness of Jeff's black ride goes beyond the dimensions and starts at the front fork – the speedometer is attached to the left lower leg. Jeff says he did it that way for two reasons. "First, I've never seen anyone else put one there. Second, it means there's no speedometer cable running from the wheel up to the bars to add clutter to the motorcycle."

Anyone who walks up to this bike from the right will assume Jeff left off the rear brake. But Jeff figured that after paying a thousand dollars per wheel, "It's pretty stupid to cover up the wheel with the brake assembly on the right and the drive sprocket on the left."

Jeff's answer to this visual dilemma is to use the rear chain sprocket on the left side for both sprocket and brake rotor. The Performance Machine brake caliper rides in a caliper bracket that Jeff designed, carved from a billet of aluminum by his friends at AARC Engineering. The result is a rear wheel free of visual distractions on the right side. While Jeff was making the sprocket do two jobs he decided to make the caliper bracket do three by designing it to function as an axle spacer and part of the license plate bracket.

The wheel itself is carved from aluminum by RC Components and measures 16 inches in diameter and six inches across, wide enough

ABOVE Large, 96-cubic-inch S&S V-twin inhales through a model G carburetor and exhales into a pair of Samson Big Guns Shorty exhaust pipes. Many Softails use two Fat Bob tanks, though Jeff chose a single, stretched tank with flush-mount cap.

RIGHT Twenty-one-inch front wheel and 38 degree rake give Jeff's bike a sense of motion, like it's already moving or at least ready to lunge ahead. Note the speedo on the fork's lower leg and the headlight housing with the long pointed shape.

for a 200 series Avon tire, currently the widest motorcycle tire manufactured. If the rear fender looks a bit unusual, it could be because it was designed originally for a boat trailer. Jeff took the unusual fender and mounted it close to the tire in a unique fashion. Instead of bolting the fender to the frame with massive fender struts, Jeff attached it to the swingarm so that it moves up and down with the tire.

Normally the rear of the seat is supported by the fender. The moving fender made that an unworkable solution. Jeff's answer is the custom solo seat seen here, with a small passenger pillion of his own design. The pillion is part of an oversize metal plate. When Jeff wants to carry a passenger he simply slides the pillion plate into a small opening behind the solo seat where it is supported by slots anchored to the frame.

Just ahead of the seat is the very long gas tank, stretched by the metal smiths at AARC to match the frame. The front fender is a modified Harley-Davidson item designed for a 21-inch front wheel. The wheel is supported by a 41mm fork assembly and slowed by a pair of Performance Machine brake calipers squeezing 10-inch rotors.

A rowdy bike needs a rowdy engine and Jeff chose a 96-cubic-inch stump puller from S&S with a 3-5/8 inch bore and a 4-5/8 inch stroke.

Just in case it didn't have enough power, Jeff had the S&S heads ported to flow more air and then installed an S&S camshaft with .562 inches of lift and 269 degrees of duration. The carburetor is the larger, Model G, from S&S while the exhaust pipes are Big Guns from Samson.

Behind the torque monster motor is a five-speed transmission with a polished case outside and James gears inside. Connecting the engine and transmission is another of those not-quite-socially-acceptable features that Jeff is so proud of. A three inch BDL primary belt used in place of the stock chain, contained in an open housing that Jeff designed to work with the design of the wheels.

If you ask Jeff about the graphics, he explains, "there may be hundreds of thousands of black Harley-Davidsons, but I've never seen one with graphics like these." The black paint is the work of Ted Cordts at Bootleg Paint in Chino, California. For the unusual graphics Jeff started with a sketch of a tribal design that's similar to some tattoos he'd seen. Steve Vanderman at Bootleg painted the graphics based on Jeff's drawing.

Jeff Beebe set out to build a unique bike and it worked. In all the parking lots at all the events, he's never seen a custom Harley quite as long, or quite as rowdy as his extra-long Softail with the big motor and the tribal graphics.

DONNIE SMITH PROFILE

Fans of Donnie Smith may not be surprised to learn that one of our best-known customizers started life on a farm in rural Minnesota. Today, Donnie acknowledges this agricultural upbringing as the environment in which he learned his basic mechanical skills. His natural ability to fix things like a broken combine were enhanced when he was sent to a high school which specialized in farming and machine maintenance. Donnie shone at subjects like motor mechanics but also learned about sheet metal work and welding, topics that would prove very useful in a few years' time.

It was after high school and a stint in the army that Donnie's natural bent for machines led him to the local drag strip outside his new home of Minneapolis, Minnesota. Donnie soon found himself part of a successful drag racing team campaigning a Willy's Gasser. By 1971 Donnie and his racing partners were earning a good living from tuning and fabrication work.

The first Smith Bros. and Fetrow shop was designed as a place to build complete cars for other racers, and thus help the three partners pay for their own drag racing habit. The first motorcycle work was done simply as a favor to a friend. But, as Donnie says, "It just seemed to snowball from there." Within a few years motorcycles and motorcycle-related projects occupied all the space in the shop. Eventually the race car had to go, in order to make way for even more motorcycles.

In the slang of the times, Smith Brothers and Fetrow was a chopper shop, and a very successful one at that. Looking back, it seems Donnie was always there behind the counter, smiling and talking with customers. Yet, he still found time to design and build a number of high-profile bikes for himself and some innovative products for the industry. Many of those Donnie Smith designed frames, forks and smaller pieces were manufactured in the shop and then sold through custom outlets all over the country.

When the modified motorcycle market went soft in the mid-1980s Donnie and his two partners decided to change with the times and quietly closed their business. After taking a break, Donnie gravitated into the small garage at his house. With a bit

of work the garage became a workshop and various one-off bikes began to roll out of the front door. Though it was never really big enough, the garage became smaller and smaller as more and more people came to ask Donnie to build them a new custom motorcycle.

Today, Donnie manages a crew of four and a constantly ringing telephone in a fairly large commercial building located in Blaine, Minnesota. One oversize bay is designed for fabrication work and the mock-up of bikes in progress. On the other side of the wall two very meticulous mechanics handle engine work and final assembly. In addition, the shop contains a small machine area, office and front counter.

Bike projects range from simple rake and stretch jobs to complete turn-key bikes. At any one time there are at least two bikes mocked-up and waiting for sheet metal pieces, and another one or two undergoing final assembly.

Donnie's relatively new relationship with Chrome Specialties, as a designer and builder for in-house products, means more work of all kinds for the shop. It's like having one more, very important, customer who requires complete bikes and a steady stream of prototype parts.

The heavy workload and frequent travel to events makes for a very busy Donnie Smith. Sometimes, especially during busy times of the year, the hours get rather long. To watch him move about the shop, encouraging the lead mechanic, then discussing the shape of a fender with his fabricator, before taking another phone call, it's difficult to imagine Donnie Smith doing anything else.

Part mechanic and part artist, Donnie Smith combines his strong mechanical background with a good sense of proportion and design.

6 RUBBER RIDES

WHEN HARLEY-DAVIDSON CREATED THE FIRST FXR MODEL LATE IN 1981, THEY COMBINED THE RUBBER ISOLATING SYSTEM, ALREADY USED IN THE DRESSER LINE, WITH THE LOOKS OF THE SUPER GLIDE. THE BIKES WERE AT FIRST CALLED SUPER GLIDE II BUT SOON EVOLVED INTO THEIR OWN LINE.

A FEW DIEHARD TRADITIONALISTS THOUGHT THE FXR MODELS TOO MODERN. FOR THEM, THERE WERE STILL SHOVELHEAD BIKES FOR SALE THAT LOOKED THE WAY HARLEYS SHOULD WITH ENGINES BOLTED DIRECTLY TO THE FRAME. A FEW YEARS LATER THE SOFTAIL BIKES WERE UNVEILED. ANOTHER SOLID, TRADITIONAL BIKE WITH A SOLID-MOUNTED ENGINE. RIDERS WITH ENOUGH IMAGINATION TO TRY OUT AN FXR, HOWEVER, SOON DISCOVERED THAT THE RUBBER MOUNTING SYSTEM LEFT THE BEST PARTS OF THE HARLEY EXPERIENCE INTACT.

THOUGH ONE OF THESE BIKES MIGHT SHAKE A LITTLE AT IDLE, EVERYTHING SMOOTHES OUT AS SOON AS YOU DROP IT IN GEAR AND LET OUT THE CLUTCH. YOU DON'T HAVE TO FIND THE "SWEET SPOT" – WHERE THE VIBRATIONS OF THE BIG V-TWIN ARE MINIMIZED ENOUGH TO ALMOST DISAPPEAR. WITHOUT REGARD FOR THE BAD VIBRATIONS, YOU CAN JUST RIDE AND RIDE, AT ANY SPEED.

HARLEY-DAVIDSON RETHOUGHT THE RUBBER-MOUNTED CONCEPT AND INTRODUCED THE DYNA LINE. WITH LOOKS REMINISCENT OF THE OLD SHOVELHEAD BIKES THE DYNA USES A SIMPLER RUBBER MOUNTING SYSTEM THAT WORKS JUST AS WELL (DEPENDING ON WHO YOU ASK) AS THE VENERABLE FXR MOUNTING SYSTEM.

WHAT THESE BIKES ALL HAVE IN COMMON IS SOME KIND OF RUBBER MOUNTING SYSTEM FOR THE ENGINE. APART FROM THAT, EACH BIKE USES A DIFFERENT COMBINATION OF FRAME, WHEEL DESIGN AND PAINT JOB TO ACHIEVE A LOOK ALL ITS OWN.

RIGHT Starting with a frame and fairing from Arlen Ness, Mark Shadley created a unique custom motorcycle that combines sophistication with flash, and speed with comfort.

ABOVE RIGHT The 130x18 inch front tire mounts to a Perewitz billet rim. Mid-glide fork assembly with painted lower legs supports a single brake caliper and rotor mounted on the left, which leaves the right side open to view.

FAR RIGHT By putting the electric fuel pump under the seat and the wiring harness inside the frame, Mark was able to create a neat engine installation. Note the polished and painted fins and chrome primary cover.

A 'LINER FROM THE SHADLEY BROTHERS

Part of the infamous Shadley Brothers partnership in Whitman, Massachusetts, Mark Shadley loves motorcycles. Sportsters, FXRs and a wide variety of customs, Mark has built them all. What Mark really loves, however, is a bike that combines the good looks of the best customs with the power of a true hot rod.

For his new bike Mark decided it was time to come in from the cold. The new bikes from Arlen Ness, what Arlen calls his "Luxury Liners," caught Mark's eye. "I was looking for a more comfortable bike," explains Mark. "With a fairing and a set of bags. When I saw how nice those 'Liners looked, I decided I had to have one."

Mark didn't want to build just any old motorcycle. While the recent trend is for big motors with nearly 100 or more cubic inches, Mark thought he could get his horsepower in a different way. Instead of bolting in an engine with huge cubic inches, he decided to make a smaller engine perform like a big one – with the addition of a turbocharger kit from Aerocharger.

The Aerocharger kits come complete with the turbo, a Mikuni carburetor, the small intercooler, the correct camshaft and all necessary plumbing. The trouble is, the kits are designed for a stock Harley-Davidson, not an Arlen Ness Dyna chassis with a five-inch stretch and one of Arlen's fairings.

Mark, however, is both a capable mechanic and a talented fabricator – the ideal person to make the finished bike look like the turbo kit was designed for it.

The start of the turbo adaptation actually began inside the motor. Mark installed stock Harley-Davidson flywheels in new, polished STD cases. On the other end of the connecting rods are 3-1/2 inch Wiseco pistons with extra-thick crowns to better withstand the pressure and heat of turbocharging. The Harley heads received Black Diamond valves, operated by the Aerocharger camshaft.

Mark figured that a nicely installed turbo installation could bring benefits beyond mere horsepower. The turbo and assorted plumbing could add a visual element to the bike. Thus Mark spared no expense on the installation. The turbo heat shield, the chrome exhaust pipe and most of the brackets used to mount the turbo and intercooler were all fabricated in the Shadley Brothers shop.

The rest of the engine is equally detailed: with hexed, painted and polished cylinders, polished and painted heads, camshaft and primary covers from Arlen Ness, and rocker box covers from Dave Perewitz. Bolted directly to the back of the engine is the polished case for the five-speed transmission, equipped with chrome-plated top and side covers. A stock belt drive takes the power from the five-speed transmission to the Perewitz/Sullivan billet aluminum rear wheel.

Instead of opting for a super-wide rear tire, Mark used a modest 140X18-inch Avon tire at the back and 130X18 in front, mounted on another Perewitz billet wheel. Supporting the front wheel are the painted lower legs, which slide up and down on 39mm tubes mounted in Arlen Ness billet triple trees. On the left side Mark installed a four-piston Arlen Ness caliper coupled to a stainless-steel rotor cut in the same pattern as the billet wheels.

The rest of the bike is mostly Luxury Liner, as interpreted by Mark Shadley. Which is to say that Mark used fenders from Jesse James, a stretched Arlen Ness gas tank and a seat from Danny Gray, all mounted with Shadley Brothers brackets. Mark did nearly all the work on this bike, even the wiring. Most of the switches are located on the bars, though the wiring is routed inside the Arlen Ness handle bars. The turbo installation requires a certain amount of extra hardware, like the electric fuel pump, which Mark hid under the seat with the ignition coils and the battery.

A wild bike needs a wild paint job and this one started with the application of a purple base color at the Cycle Fab shop. But what really sets this bike apart are the graphics done by the talented Nancy Brooks.

The finished bike is like a Cadillac with a blown big block. This extremely bright and very fast Dyna offers that rare combination of speed and comfort. And like a good Cadillac, the bike has given Mark over 3,000 trouble-free miles. "It's one of the nicest bikes to ride that I've ever built," says Mark. Yet, in the next breath he explains that the bike is for sale. Not because of some hidden failing, but because no matter how nice the current bike is, there's always another one out there rattling around in Mark's brain. We all do crazy things for love.

BELOW The air plenum for the turbo system gave Mark a good place to put the Shadley Brothers logo. Polished fins and chrome-plated billet covers help create an engine every bit as bright as the rest of the bike.

DANNY BUILDS A DYNA

When Danny Gray, manufacturer of custom seats for Harley-Davidsons, decided it was time for a new ride, he called on a man who is both a good friend and well-known custom bike builder. Dave Perewitz is actually as much a talented designer as he is a builder, able to conceive motorcycles that are both visually exciting and fully functional. Though some people might have started with a used bike or an aftermarket frame, Danny asked Dave Perewitz to go out and order a brand new Dyna Glide from the local dealer.

Dave's Cycle Fab crew began the project by taking things off the motorcycle until they were left with a bare frame. In order to get the length called for in David's design, five inches were added to the frame between the seat and the neck. At the same time the angle of the neck was changed from about 30 to 38 degrees.

The hardest part of the whole job involved moving the battery inboard. Unlike the earlier FXR chassis, which carries its battery in the center of the frame, the Harley-Davidson engineers located the Dyna battery on the outside under the seat. Creating a bike with a sleek

BELOW The rake of the frame really puts the 19-inch Perewitz wheel out in front. Note the Headwinds headlight and the small panels crafted to fill the void where the gas tank drops down over the frame tubes.

profile meant relocation of the battery to an inboard position, which proved to be harder than you might think.

Making room for the battery meant removing structural members under the seat, crafting a new inboard battery box and then re-engineering the entire area to replace the lost strength.

Once the frame work was completed work could begin on the sleek sheet metal shapes designed to fit the trimmed and stretched frame.

By moving the battery inside it became possible to fabricate a wraparound sheet metal cover that looks like an oil tank. Creating a gas tank with a long sensuous shape required more fabrication.

The front fender, from Jesse James, wraps close to the 19 inch Avon tire. The rear tire is another Avon gumball, one size larger than stock, covered by a modified Harley-Davidson fender with a fabricated Cycle Fab taillight. After all the fabrication came the molding, or smoothing

At the center of every custom Harley beats a V-twin heart. Even though they were dealing with a brand new bike, David thought a little improvement was called for in the horsepower department. East Coast engine man Wayne Lofton decided to increase the horsepower without changing the engine's basic displacement. Thus the Harley-Davidson cases, flywheels, cylinders and heads were all retained. New are the Wiseco angle-top pistons, the Crane camshaft and the shape of the ports in the Harley heads. A QuickSilver carburetor takes the place of the stock Keihin, while a pair of Bub pipes were chosen to replace the stock, staggered duals.

Externally, the engine is fully polished, with hexed cylinders, Perewitz rocker boxes and Arlen Ness primary and cam covers. The five-speed transmission offers more of the same - a polished case filled with back-cut RevTech gears and a Perewitz top cover.

If a classic Perewitz custom needs to be long, it also needs to be low. At the back David swapped the stock shock absorbers for a pair of 11 inch Works shocks with aluminum bodies. In front, billet triple trees clamp the factory fork tubes and painted lower legs, equipped with shorter Progressive springs.

More of the stock parts were swapped for the latest offerings from the aftermarket during the final assembly. The handle bars and grips are from Arlen Ness, while the headlight is a beautiful billet piece from Headwinds. The custom seat is of course from Danny Gray, the man Dave Perewitz calls, "the finest seat maker in the world."

Looking over Danny's new bike, your eye naturally follows the line from gas tank to the side cover; from side cover to fender. Like most Perewitz designs, this one "flows," partly because the bike is long, partly because the sheet metal shapes are designed to accentuate the length and blend together.

The completion of the new bike means that when Danny rides around Daytona or Sturgis, he isn't just riding on any old motorcycle. Instead, Danny Gray shows up on a very red, very clean David Perewitz designed Dyna - a two-wheeled sculpture powered by a hot rod Harley motor.

LEFT Increases in compression, breathing and ignition ensure that this 80-cubic-inch motor performs much better than its stock counterpart. The polished fins contrast nicely with the red paint on the factory heads and cylinders. Even the CompuFire starter is polished to a bright shine.

BELOW The bottom three fins were cut off the cylinders prior to the polishing. Though many of the current custom Harleys run forward controls, this Dyna retains the stock "mid-glide" position.

of any visible seams and welds. Application of the very red House of Kolor paint was done by Russ and Dave at Cycle Fab, though the graphics are the work of Nancy Brooks.

These "Stalker" billet aluminum rims are more of David's design work, manufactured and distributed by Sullivan Brothers in Hanson, Massachusetts. The four-piston brake calipers, carved from billet by Arlen Ness, provide the slow while adding to the show.

FULL SPEED AHEAD

The Harley-Davidson aftermarket is running faster and faster. Each year is better than the last, with more customers, more ideas, more money and more new products than anyone would have predicted just a few years ago. The creative individuals who design and build the parts that fill the catalogs are all working overtime, trying to fill the demand for new parts and accessories.

Dave Perewitz is no exception. Since beginning his association with Bobby Sullivan at Sullivan Brothers, David has cranked out a whole range of wheels, pulleys, engine covers and a complete fork assembly. It's one of those jobs that's never done, because as soon as you finish one new product, there's the need to improve or add to a design you did a year ago.

When David's friend Tommy D. approached him to build a new bike, David saw it as a chance to try out some of his new prototype products. Through good timing or good karma, Tommy turned out to be the first person with the "new line" from Dave Perewitz.

The new line includes the prototype 18-inch billet wheels used at either end, carved from billet aluminum by the Carriage Works. The front wheel is supported by David's fork assembly consisting of smooth lower legs that work with factory 41mm fork tubes and internal components. The mid-glide triple trees that clamp those tubes are also part of the evolving line of Perewitz parts.

The front brake is made up of a single, four-piston GMA caliper matched to a floating rotor. The real news in the brake department, however, is at the back of the bike. Factory bikes and most custom machines put the rear brake on the right, while in the case of the new Perewitz prototype brake and pulley assembly, the brake is on the left. The caliper is anchored to the swingarm and clamps a rotor that bolts to the inside of the rear wheel pulley.

David doesn't manufacture a frame, at least not yet. The frame for the new prototype machine is a Dyna-style frame from his friend Arlen Ness. The frame that Arlen shipped from California to Massachusetts came with five inches of stretch and a 35 degree fork angle. To spice things up a little David had the swingarm chrome plated, then masked off the front half and had it sand blasted so that part of the swingarm would have enough texture to hold paint.

The gas tanks and center "dash," which seem long even for a David Perewitz bike, are the work of Jed, chief metal-man in the Cycle Fab shop. Both front and rear fenders came from Jesse James, owner of West Coast Choppers and another individual who's been burning the midnight oil designing new products for the aftermarket. With the exception of the chrome-plated half of the swingarm, all the sheet metal and chassis parts are sprayed with a retina-burning yellow urethane paint from House of Kolor. Due to a mishap on one of the bike's first outings, most of the machine has actually been painted not once, but twice. The original molding and paint, as well as the second paint job, are the work of Dave's brother Donnie and Russ Keene at the Cycle Fab shop.

LEFT The trend of late is to single-sided front brakes and a rear brake on the left side. David and crew narrowed this Arlen Ness frame in the area under the seat and achieved a different look.

LEFT Engines are becoming an integral part of the bike's visual package. Note the deep blue paint which contrasts nicely with both the polished fins and the yellow paint.

TOP Dave Perewitz likes his tanks long and concave on the bottom, separated by a smooth dash without any gauges.

ABOVE The critter on the tank is a hamster. The owner of this yellow ride is a member of that hallowed group of fun loving, custom bike enthusiasts. Side covers are new, crafted to fit the narrowed frame.

The V-twin that resides below the long stretched gas tanks is a 96-cubic-inch mill that David bought complete but unassembled from S&S. Before assembly could begin David sent the cases, cylinders and heads out to be polished, then had the fins on the cylinders and heads masked off so both could be painted a deep blue. Once the paint was dry Jim Thompson began assembling the parts into a running whole. Jim chose a Crane camshaft for the big S&S engine.

Perewitz rocker boxes cap the S&S heads, while the cam and primary covers are from Arlen Ness. The new coil bracket on the left side with CompuFire coils is another of David's new products. Samson pipes stretch back past the polished five-speed transmission, equipped with the new billet top cover. The transmission side cover is really part of David's new hydraulic clutch assembly, powered by a Billet Concepts master cylinder on the handle bars.

The new yellow bike is a fast ride, zero to 60 in less than five seconds. That's almost as fast as the Harley-Davidson aftermarket, which has gone from stone-dead to full-speed-ahead in less than 10 years. If the number of new parts on David's yellow bike is any indication of the rate of change for this emerging industry, we should all hang on tight, because it's going to be a wild ride.

ABOVE The yellow Dyna uses a 96 cubic inch S&S mill for power, equipped with a Crane cam and Samson exhaust pipes. Rocker boxes are David's own, as are the transmission side and top covers.

BUILT FOR SHOW
– AND GO

By definition, most custom bikes are built for show. Riding is limited to short jaunts, or no jaunts at all. Andreas "Fietje" Friedrich, on the other hand, wanted a radical ride he could use for touring. The bike had firstly to be legal for use on German roads, and secondly to have a radical look all its own.

The Harley-Davidson FXR frame makes a good foundation for a bike that is both fast and easy to ride. The rubber mounting means the engine can vibrate without shaking and wearing out the rider. With the battery located under the seat, this same frame provides a sleek profile that customizers like Andreas can easily improve upon.

Though it's fairly common to "stretch" a frame and thus enhance the long, lean profile, Andreas stretched his to the limit and beyond. The area between the neck and the seat is now five inches longer than it was stock. At the same time Andreas increased the fork angle to 36 degrees. Not content with a bike that was five inches longer, he then had the swingarm extended an additional three inches.

To complement the bike's long lines Andreas stretched a stock one-piece gas tank to fit the longer frame. At the back, a fabricated tail-dragging fender covers the spoked wheel and reaches nearly to the ground. Under the seat is another fabricated item some people might miss. Stock FXRs have an oil tank that protrudes into the area just behind the rear cylinder. To give the bike a more open look the oil tank on Andreas' FXR is contained within the frame so the area behind the cylinder and above the starter is much more open.

Though nearly all the FXRs on the road, both stock and custom, use hydraulic front forks, Andreas chose to use a springer fork, fully chrome plated and shortened two inches to help lower the bike. The Progressive shocks used at the rear are likewise shorter than stock so both ends of the radical red ride sit very close to the asphalt.

The red rocket's heart is an 80-cubic-inch V-twin made up of Harley-Davidson flywheels housed in polished factory engine cases. The aluminum Harley cylinders have also been polished and then

painted, and house Wiseco 3-½ inch pistons. Cylinder heads from the king of porting, Jerry Branch, top off each cylinder, the Manley valves operated by a Head Quarters camshaft. An SU constant velocity carburetor feeds gas and air while a pair of Bub pipes provide a non-restrictive exit to the atmosphere.

Immediately behind the V-twin is the factory five-speed transmission, connected to the motor by a Primo belt drive. Power leaving the transmission passes through the Barnett clutch to the drive chain and on to the fat, 170x18-inch rear tire. To slow all this horsepower down, Andreas chose to use a factory-style caliper in front and an eight-piston aluminum caliper from Hot Shot on the rear wheel.

When it came time to decide on the paint Andreas never hesitated. "Red, red, red", he told the painter. "And when you've finished making it red, I want flames in bright yellow with a little orange, offset with blue pinstripes." The final bits and pieces needed to finish the bike came from a variety of sources, all designed to complement the rest of the machine. The solo seat is from Gido, the grips are from Arlen Ness and the billet taillight is from Pro One.

Once completed Andreas found the new machine made a good road bike. Good enough for extensive tours of the continent. During one of those tours, to the Ibiza Bike Week festivities, Andreas won Best of Show with his extra-long, extra-red "sport touring" machine. All of which goes to show that the creative builder can indeed craft a machine that goes just as well as it shows.

BELOW Crane HI-4 ignition fires a high-output coil hidden behind the factory cover. Note the polished cases, and the neatly polished and painted cylinders and heads. Oil coolers mount to the frame's lower downtubes.

LEFT Long tank isn't just stretched, it's stretched and shaped to arch over the chrome and painted rocker boxes. *Horst Rösler*

BELOW Tiller style handle bars mount to short risers. Billet grips and chrome switch housing help to clean up the bars.

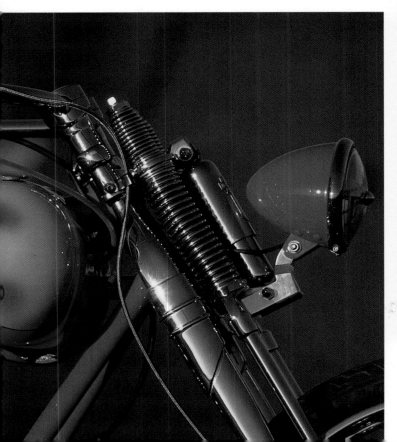

FLYING TIGER

High-performance brakes and suspension make this a more functional Harley-Davidson FXR. Note the unusual oil tank and trim front fender. *Photo: Horst Rösler*

No belt drive or factory swingarms here. WiWo truss-type swingarm uses eccentric axle adjusters. Chain drive leaves more room for the 140x17-inch tire. *Photo: Horst Rösler*

Building a custom Harley in Germany can be tough. It isn't the building that's so different to anywhere else, it's the numerous rules an owner must comply with in order to license a modified motorcycle. If you succeed, however, all the German roads, including the Autobahn, become part of your playpen.

German engineer Christoph Madaus from Cologne is a man with more than one custom Harley. A man with both the skills necessary to do most of the work on his own motorcycles, and the persistence to see that the end results pass the strict German laws. With a background in mechanical engineering, Chris' improvements to the bike are focused primarily on function, though form and function are closely linked for most Harley-Davidson owners.

To provide more power for Autobahn use Chris made a series of refinements to the 80-cubic-inch V-twin, starting with the addition of an SU constant-velocity carburetor and Hypercharger air cleaner. The precision of single-fire ignition is handled by the Dyna S ignition system. Instead of hiding the high-output coils behind a cover, Chris

left them hanging out in the breeze on the bike's left side, along with the voltage regulator.

If the Germans are known for engineering and finely crafted luxury automobiles, the Italians are known for their motorcycle fork assemblies. The Ceriani name is well respected all over the world as the manufacturer of extremely high-quality fork assemblies intended for both street and competition use. For the front of his FXR Chris chose a 43mm Ceriani fork assembly mounted in aluminum Ceriani triple trees.

By making his own brackets Chris was able to mount two, four-piston Performance Machine brake calipers to the lower legs of the Italian fork assembly. The fabricated brackets locate the calipers where they can best clamp the large-diameter floating rotors. The front wheel combines an Akront aluminum rim with a wheel and hub from WiWo. Wrapping the rim is a Bridgestone 100X18-inch tire.

This international motorcycle with the Italian forks and Japanese tires uses French shock absorbers from Fournales. Unlike conventional shocks wound with a spring, the Fournales units use a cushion of high-pressure air to support the back of the bike. The lower end of these slick shock absorbers bolts to a massive aluminum swingarm with eccentric axle adjusters made by WiWo. The swingarm

supports a somewhat unusual rear wheel made up of a WiWo hub and disc coupled to a Akront rim. Mounted to the rim is a 140X17-inch Bridgestone tire. Instead of the factory belt, Chris chose chain drive to the rear wheel.

Chris' abilities extend beyond mere assembly or even machining of aluminum parts. The fabricated front fender is another of his creations, as is the small air dam bolted to the frame behind the front wheel. The rear fender is a modified factory fender, the gas tank too is a made-in-Milwaukee item.

The handle bars mount to the top triple trees with short risers, both the bars and the risers have been modified so all the wiring runs inside. Rather than use a conventional dash, Chris installed a digital display. Turn signals have been located at either end of the handle bars, just outboard from the billet grips.

The turquoise paint job is by Nicolay in Cologne, while the airbrush work is by Becker Design in Nieder-Olm. The Flying Tiger logo on the tank brings back images of brave men in leather jackets flying high-performance aircraft. What better image for a high-performance motorcycle designed to fly low over the Autobahn, piloted by a certain leather-clad engineer from Cologne?

ABOVE Serious brakes: twin four-piston calipers are coupled with large diameter floating rotors. Eighteen-inch-tire mounts to a Akront rim bolted to a disc-style wheel.

ABOVE LEFT High-performance coils mount in the area normally covered by a side cover. Voltage regulator mounts just behind the coils.

A FAMILY AFFAIR

It might be genetic that both Richard Seals and his daughter Debbie make their living in the airline industry. And it might be Nature who dictated both would ride motorcycles. But it's strictly luck that both ride customized Harley-Davidson FXRs.

Luck in this case takes the name of Grady Pfeiffer, diehard custom enthusiast and sales representative for various aftermarket companies. A few years back Debbie was minding her own business, riding along on the streets of LA when she met Grady and friends, all riding decidedly non-stock Milwaukee two-wheelers. A friendship formed and more motorcycle rides followed. Before long Debbie was admiring the customized bikes and asking Grady for advice on customizing hers.

"Debbie was riding this stock FXR," explains Grady. "It was OK but it had all the stock stuff on it. I lowered it for her and added a little Ness fairing and side covers."

Now, Debbie is a fully independent woman, but when father Richard Seals heard that some guy was "improving" her FXR, he decided to stop by for a friendly chat. Instead of disapproving of his daughter's choice of friends, Richard came away from that first meeting with a new friend and a fascination for this idea of removing parts from a motorcycle to make it more appealing. When Richard considered his own stock FXRT, with saddle bags and tour pack, he realized that his bike had a lot of room for improvement.

In a nutshell, that's how the father-daughter team of Richard and Debbie Seals came to ride a pair of very clean and very sanitary FXRs. For Debbie, the next step-up came when the engine on her FXR gave trouble. Bartels Harley-Davidson pulled the engine out to repair the bottom end, and while the engine was out Grady and his friend Howard Stubbins took the bike home to their shop.

Debbie's bike was soon just a pile of parts. Once they had the frame bare, Grady and Howard took it over to Kevin Seawright, who increased the fork rake to 38 degrees and molded all the welds. Next, the frame, swingarm and lower legs were painted black. In place of the factory wheels a new pair of billet aluminum hoops were installed, a 16-inch at the back and a 19-inch in front. The front rotor shares the design seen in the rims, coupled to a chrome-plated factory-style caliper.

Bolted to the frame is the trick rear fender with the unique light assembly, done by Famart Welding. The front fender is simply a molded factory fender. Likewise the gas tank, which resembles a stock tank minus the dash, with a flush-mount cap. Over the whole thing is a very bright paint job by Phil Stadden in Torrance, California. Danny Gray supplied the seat while the Arlen Ness catalog supplied the bars and many of the accessories.

As Grady explains it, Richard's bike was a little more work, "He started with an FXRT, so there was all that touring stuff to consider. And he wanted to do some of the work himself." Eventually the partially completed bike ended up in Grady and Howard's shop so Howard could do the engine work and Grady could put it all back together again.

Similarities between the two bikes include the rake angle of 38 degrees, the modified factory sheet metal and their basic "attitude." Differences in Richard's bike include the chrome-plated GMA brakes,

LEFT Debbie and her father Richard consider themselves lucky: both love motorcycles, both ride great-looking FXRs and both love to spend the first week of August with thousands of friends in Sturgis, South Dakota.

ABOVE A "hot rod" 80 with a mild boost in compression and improved breathing give Debbie's FXR more snort when the light turns green.

the polished and painted factory wheels, and the candy red paint used on both the sheet metal and the frame.

While both bikes use "leaned on" 80-cubic-inch motors for power, Richard's is the more radical of the two. Assembled by Howard, his bike uses a Crane camshaft with .600 inches of lift, mated to 10.3:1 compression Dave Mackie ported heads. Debbie's Bartels-assembled V-Twin on the other hand relies on the more common and less radical Sifton 141 cam with .480 inches of lift, working in harmony with the 9:1 compression heads ported by Fast Eddie. For carburetors, Bartels chose to stay with the stock CV carb while Howard picked a butterfly-style Series E mixer from S&S. Both use Bub pipes.

Externally, both engines use painted and polished cylinders combined with high-quality chrome-plated cam and primary covers. Differences include the fully polished cases used on Richard's bike and the different air cleaners – Richard's uses an S&S air cleaner while Debbie's V-twin breathes through a factory filter.

Because they live in different cities and spend most of their working time in the air, it's hard for Richard and Debbie to get together, even for occasions like Christmas. The event that both attend religiously, however, is the annual motorcycle rally in Sturgis, South Dakota. One week with plenty of time for friends, family and riding in the hills. In fact, when last seen in Sturgis there was another, younger daughter in the group. Debbie's younger sister was riding a Sportster at the time, but then it was her first trip to Sturgis and she probably hadn't met Grady yet.

BELOW A hotter, hot rod 80, with 10.3 to 1 compression, a high-lift cam and S&S Super E carburetor.

PROWLING AUSTRALIA

The current enthusiasm for V-twins and the shortage of bikes in many Harley dealerships throughout the world has led to a thriving "clone" business. Anyone and everyone is setting up shop to become a motorcycle manufacturer. In small quantities the process isn't too tough. Just take your pick of an aftermarket frame and engine, add accessories, assemble with care(?) and put your own John Henry on the gas tank.

When the Australian Flood family decided to build a better V-twin however, they approached it differently. Trevor and Gary Flood are both retired racers and spend much of their time tuning suspension systems for competition bikes all over Australia. Their father Bert, another retired racer, works as a consultant to the motorcycle industry.

Together they set out to build a better V-twin motorcycle, one that takes advantage of the V-twin power and torque, without the traditional limitations in ground clearance, handling and weight. The result of their efforts is the Prowler, a uniquely Australian V-Twin motorcycle that combines the power and torque of a V-twin engine with the light weight and handling normally associated with bikes from Europe or Japan.

Though the Prowler might look at first like just another Softail, a closer look reveals that instead of using two shocks under the transmission, this "Softail" relies on a single White Power shock hidden under the seat. The unusual frame is fabricated in Australia from chrome-moly tubing to specifications and drawings provided by Trevor and Gary Flood. Up front the well supported neck area supports an upside down White Power fork assembly. The net result is a very strong, lightweight frame with more ground clearance and suspension travel than anything to come out of Milwaukee or the aftermarket.

ABOVE V-twins and twisty roads don't have to be mutually exclusive. With adequate ground clearance and suspension travel the Prowler is a big bike that actually handles the curves with ease.

ABOVE Sourced mostly in Australia, the Prowler combines modern looks and high-quality components with a traditional V-twin engine. Note the unique "sheet metal" including the aerodynamic front fender and sleek rear inner fender.

RIGHT Taillight housing mounts to the rear inner fender while the turn signals bolt to the aluminum seat-strut. Wherever possible Trevor specified lightweight parts manufactured in Australia.

If the Prowler is designed for speed, it's also designed for comfort. Rather than bolt the engine and transmission directly to the frame, the Flood-designed frame uses a Dyna-style rubber mounting system for the engine and transmission. The use of a Dyna drivetrain has another advantage. Dyna five-speed transmissions mount the oil tank for the engine under the transmission, not under the seat. Production Prowlers will use a transmission case cast from magnesium as a means of further reducing total weight.

The twin goals of light weight and high quality are both met by producing the bodywork in-house. The gas tank, "ducktail," fenders and side covers are all produced from either Kevlar or carbon fiber. A neat aluminum housing mounts the speedometer and tachometer in the center of the tank. In order to keep as much of the production as possible in Australia, many of the parts that can't be produced in house are sourced to local firms.

The 88 cubic inch engine is the one item that Trevor and Gary couldn't find in Australia. The S&S components are, however, assembled into a running whole by local engine man Graham Smythe. For exhaust a stainless steel two-into-one system from Staintune, another Australian company, was chosen. A primary belt is used to carry the power to the transmission where close-ratio Andrews gears deliver the torque to the output pulley. Another belt carries the power to the unusual 17-inch rear wheel. Like the frame, the wheels are designed by the Flood brothers and produced locally. The spun aluminum design was chosen as a good combination of strength and light weight. Both wheels measure 17 inches in diameter, the front is 3.5 inches wide while the rear is a full 4.5 inches in width.

A pair of six piston Performance Machine calipers and huge 13.5 inch floating rotors give the Prowler brakes as good as those found on any Ninja or Ducati. Because the front brakes do nearly all the braking on a hard stop the rear brakes use a single four-piston PM caliper and a smaller rotor.

The finished machine is known as the T38, T for Trevor Flood and 38 because that was father Bert's racing number. Equipped with world-class brakes and suspension the Australian V-twin hot rod succeeds in combining the torque of a V-twin in a light chassis that provides excellent handling. The Flood's weight saving program was so successful that the finished bike weighs less than a Sportster. Never satisfied, Trevor plans to cast the brake calipers, as well as a transmission case, from magnesium and further reduce the weight on the production bikes.

Speaking of production, the T38 will only be produced in limited numbers, on the order of 200 units per year, starting in mid-1998. With the power and appeal of a V-twin and the back-road prowess of a crotch rocket the T38 is Australia's first Super Bike.

LEFT A nice touch is the aluminum dash that mounts the speedo, warning lights and tachometer into the top of the gas tank.

DAVE PEREWITZ PROFILE

Dave Perewitz seems like a pretty happy-go-lucky person. At events he always seems to be laughing and telling jokes, the loud Boston accent carrying across the room. Yet, underneath that jovial exterior is a thoughtful custom bike builder. A man who worked hard to achieve a high level of recognition, and who works equally hard now developing new products sold under his name.

Dave's first foray into professional Harley-Davidson painting and repair came early, when he put up a small shop behind his father's house in the early 1970s. With help from his brother Donnie, Dave was able to paint and build a number of custom bikes each year, some of which found their way into the custom magazines of the period.

Ten years later Dave and Donnie were still at it, building and painting motorcycles and forming friendships with other builders like Arlen Ness, Donnie Smith and Don Hotop. By the early 1980s David had a larger shop and a separate retail store in Brockton, Massachusetts. As the business grew, David's wife Susan helped by keeping the books.

Today, David still owns the store in Brockton and he still does most of the fabrication and paint work at a separate shop close to the house. As he explains, "The store is nice, because all the customers go there, it's a place to do business and meet people. The store helps us keep the customers out of the shop so there's no interruption of the work."

What has changed for David is the nature of the work and who he works for. No longer do the new fabricated parts simply go onto a customer's bike and out of the door. Innovative designs, first used as part of a complete bike, turn into retail parts sold through his evolving relationship with Sullivan Brothers, or occasionally, Nempco. The other change is in the crew. Though he experiences very little turnover, there is one new face in the Cycle Fab shop - Jesse Perewitz, David's son, who always comes to help out after school.

What hasn't changed over the years is David's ability to design and produce great-looking custom motorcycles. His style has evolved with the times, yet you can usually tell a Perewitz bike by the exceptional paint and the way the whole motorcycle hangs together as a design, not just a collection of nice parts.

So if you see an ad for the new Perewitz billet wheels in a magazine, don't be tempted to think, "this Perewitz guy has it made." Despite the name recognition, the ads and the stories in the magazines, David still puts in plenty of hours each week. In a sense, bike builders are like football or baseball players. You can tell the ones who are really good at what they do, because they make it look easy.

As much a designer as builder, Dave Perewitz has a knack for building bikes that "flow" from one end to the other.

KNOWN AS DRESSERS OR BAGGERS, THERE SEEM TO BE MORE FULL-DRESS HARLEY-DAVIDSONS ON THE STREETS EACH YEAR. AND A LARGE PERCENTAGE ARE MODIFIED OR CUSTOMIZED. PERHAPS IT'S THE BABY BOOMERS GETTING OLDER AND GOING SLOWER WITH MORE COMFORT. PERHAPS THESE BIKES ARE FINALLY GETTING THE RECOGNITION THEY DESERVE AS THE CLASSIC AMERICAN ROAD BIKE.

THE PEOPLE AT HARLEY-DAVIDSON AREN'T THE ONLY ONES PARTICIPATING. ALL THE MAJOR CATALOG COMPANIES HAVE A WEALTH OF NEW PARTS DESIGNED SPECIFICALLY FOR THE BIG HARLEY. NOT JUST MORE LIGHTS AND CHROME STRIPS, BUT REAL PARTS DESIGNED TO IMPROVE THE LOOKS AND PERFORMANCE OF YOUR ROAD BIKE.

THE PARTS RUN THE GAMUT FROM LOWERING KITS TO "FILL-IN" TRIM PIECES THAT FIT BETWEEN THE BAGS AND THE FENDER AND MAKE THE BAGS SEEM MORE LIKE AN INTEGRAL PART OF THE BIKE. DRESSERS ARE BECOMING SEAMLESS AND MORE SOPHISTICATED.

THE DRESSER PHENOMENON SEEMS TO BE SUBTRACTIVE-CUSTOMIZING. PEOPLE TEND TO MODIFY AND SIMPLIFY THE BIKE BY TAKING THINGS OFF. THAT WAY THE NICE LINES AND THE GOOD BASIC DESIGN OF THESE KINGS OF THE HIGHWAY CAN SHINE THROUGH.

THERE WAS A TIME WHEN NOBODY BUT YOUR UNCLE WOULD BE CAUGHT DEAD ON A DRESSER. ANYONE UNDER 30 SAID, "HEY, THEY'RE OK FOR JOE AND MARTHA, BUT I WANT TO KEEP THE OLD STRIPPED-DOWN SHOVELHEAD." THOSE DAYS ARE GONE. MOST OF US ARE AS OLD AS OUR UNCLE JOE. IF NOT, IT DOESN'T MATTER BECAUSE DRESSERS ARE SO COOL EVERYBODY WANTS ONE.

HERE ARE FIVE BIKES: A MUCH MODIFIED ROAD KING, THREE DIFFERENT INTERPRETATIONS OF "STANDARD DRESSER CUSTOMIZING" AND A DRESSER AS SEEN THROUGH THE EYES OF ARLEN NESS.

RIGHT Joe Pro is a man who likes to have the latest ride. For the new Road King he set out to create a bike that retains the comforts of a Dresser while adding more flash, style and performance.

ABOVE RIGHT Like the rear, the front end uses a single GMA caliper and a rotor designed to match the style of the Perewitz billet wheels.

THE LATEST THING

Joe Procopio, "Joe Pro" to friends, is a man who always rides a new Harley-Davidson. "This new one is my eleventh bike in 18 years," he explains.

The new bike in question is one of Harley-Davidson's recent marketing triumphs, a Road King. Like most of his bikes, Joe bought this one at Cycle Craft Harley-Davidson in Everette, Massachusetts. Before tearing into a new bike Joe likes to put a few miles on the odometer. "It's exactly 31 miles from the dealer to the Cycle Fab shop," explains Joe with a smile. "David Perewitz teases me because whenever I bring in a bike it always has 31 miles on the clock."

Joe's relationship with Cycle Fab goes back a long way. "I hung around the shop so much and for so long," says Joe, "that David finally made me an employee."

With help from the crew, Joe stripped the new bike down to nothing but a bare frame sitting on a packing crate, surrounded by the stock fenders, wheels, drivetrain and all the other parts that make up a complete motorcycle.

It should be stated that there is nothing wrong with the stock Harley-Davidson sheet metal. The factory fenders and tanks are, in fact, of the highest quality, covered with paint that is blemish free and very durable. But it just doesn't work for Joe Pro. In place of the Milwaukee iron Joe ordered a front and rear fender from Jesse James, then asked his buddy Jed from Cycle Fab to fabricate a taillight housing and install it in the bottom of the rear fender.

While he was talking Jed into performing sheet metal miracles, Joe suggested they add extensions to the end of the factory gas tank. Jed did him one better by cutting up the tank until there was little of the original left, and then bringing it back until the tails on either side almost touch the side covers. Of course, Jed hadn't fabricated the side covers yet, but when he did they turned out well.

David suggested they paint the bike orange, "But I didn't like the idea of an orange bike," says Joe. Instead he convinced Donnie and David, the brothers Perewitz, to paint the bike in a tangelo color from House of Kolor. Not only did the boys paint the sheet metal, they went for a bit of the Euro-look by painting the headlight nacelle, fork assembly, dash and even the fender struts in the same tangelo hue. Nancy Brooks did the graphics before Donnie laid on the final clearcoats.

It may be considered heresy to build a custom bike without attending to the motor. However, remember that Joe bought the Road King with the fuel-injected engine. Consider too that he built the King before Harley-Davidson and the aftermarket came up with the innovative ways to correct the fuel curves to compensate for any engine modifications. Joe can be forgiven if the only changes he made to the motor are the Bub pipes, which still contain the full complement of packing and baffles.

This new Road King wasn't going to be some stripped-down custom and Joe wanted the bike to carry all the stock equipment. He wanted to retain the things most of us take for granted, like turn signals and switches on the handle bars. At the front, small oval clearance lights bolt to the headlight nacelle and function as unobtrusive turn signals. At the back, aftermarket clearance lights function as blinkers. Painted to match the bike they almost disappear into the rear fender struts. While the taillight is set into the fender, the license plate bracket bolts to the swingarm on the left side, "like an old rigid bike," says Joe.

For wheels Joe chose new, 16 inch aluminum assemblies from his employer Dave Perewitz, with a 130 series tire on the front and a 140 on the rear. The rear shocks are the stock length, though they bolt to a swingarm that's been inverted to drop the back of the bike about two inches. The use of the flipped swingarm and an aftermarket fork assembly up front means the whole machine sits lower than stock, but not so low that Joe worries about dragging the frame on speed bumps and driveways.

Harley-Davidson might consider the Road King a stripped dresser, but for Joe even their stripped bike had too many brackets, windshields and saddle bags. Shed of all that extra bulk, Joe's new bike looks pretty good, almost like a slightly oversize FXR. If you ask him, he says the bike is, "really great." At the same time he is making plans to build another machine, based on a new Arlen Ness frame. Why? Because for Joe, Road Kings are old hat. But now a Ness-framed custom, that's the latest thing.

BELOW Jesse James rear fender houses a Cycle Fab taillight. By painting the clearance lights and bolting them to the fender struts the rear "turn signals" become an integral part of the bike instead of an add-on.

A CANADIAN EYE OPENER

Michael Ethier hails from Maschouche, Quebec, near Montreal, but that doesn't stop him from making the long pilgrimage to Daytona for Bike Week's annual rites. One year he brought a wild Softail, more recently he showed up in Florida with a Dresser that looks as though it was white and purple before he rode it through a vat of yellow paint at high speed. You can see clearly where the blobs of yellow paint impacted against the front fender, the tanks, the side covers and the fiberglass bags. Each blob of yellow flowed back, taking the path of least resistance, stringing out into a thin strip before drying in a teardrop shape on the tank or bag.

Bob Morin from St. Hubert, Quebec, applied the white and purple paint and Sylvain Beliveau from Montreal did the very intricate graphics with an airbrush. With acres of sheet metal and fiberglass, Dressers provide the ideal canvas for a talented painter. Michael is certainly one Harley rider who understands this. But before you

accuse him of coming to Daytona with a "repainted stock Dresser," take another look at the bike.

The extensive sheet metal work includes the front fender that nearly drags the asphalt, the tanks that reach back to blend with the frame, and the thin strips of chrome plate that decorate the side covers and bags.

Daniel Lauzon from Montreal is the man responsible for the extended front fender and the tails on the tanks. While extended tanks have become fairly common, less common are the chrome rails that rise up between the top of the bags and the fender, and the shock absorber covers that you see between the fender and bag when you look at the bike from the back.

The neat little chrome strips are the work of the Bozzini Machine Shop in Montreal. Each strip was manufactured from steel before being shipped off to the chrome shop. They aren't glued on but are

ABOVE The billet rocker boxes, pushrod covers, tappet blocks and all the rest carry the Arlen Ness logo.

ABOVE The factory wheels are different colors to match the different paint on the opposite ends of the bike. Airbrush work is extremely nice, note the "stainless" trim on the edge of the windshield.

ABOVE RIGHT The factory tanks have been extended to meet the frame and side covers. Note the details in Sylvain Beliveau's airbrush work - the dripping yellow on the face of the instruments and the way the purple spears go through a "hole" in the yellow on the side of the tank.

held in place by small screws that come in from the back side.

The highly detailed V-Twin features four different colors of powder coat, contrasting with the polished fins and abundant billet. Deshaies Cycle in Montreal disassembled the engine so the various parts could be polished and/or powder coated. Arthur Tiberyan, the mechanic at Deshaies Cycle who did most of the work, installed an S&S carburetor and a pair of Bartels pipes, but left the engine otherwise stock.

Most of the engine accessories and covers are from the Arlen Ness billet aluminum line. Things like the air cleaner, lifter blocks, pushrod covers, rocker boxes, cam cover, derby and inspection covers - to name just a few - are all from Arlen's catalog.

Though there's plenty of billet aluminum on Michael's bike, he chose to retain the stock cast 16-inch wheels at both the front and the back. The factory wheels have been polished at the edge of the rim and then powder coated to match the paint on either end of the bike. Metzeler tires in stock 130/90X16-inch sizes mount to both rims.

A pair of JayBrake four-piston calipers mount to the front fork legs while the stock caliper is retained at the rear. To lower the bike in the front, the fork tubes were cut two inches. At the rear, a White Brothers kit is used to bring the back of the bike down a similar amount.

Final assembly was done at the Deshaies Cycle shop, and when it came time to choose the accessories and assorted hardware, Michael

insisted on the same high quality that was used for the engine. The bars, switches, grips and mirrors all carry the Arlen Ness logo. And though the taillight is from Arlen's catalog, the small lights – including the blinker lights that have been set into the bags – use lenses from the Custom Chrome catalog.

There are a few more things to point out on Michael's latest creation – things that might get lost in this sea of polished aluminum and multi-colored paint, like the purple cover for the re-shaped seat, done by Mister Meloche from Montreal, a man more accustomed to working on Ferraris than Harley-Davidsons. But perhaps the cleverest trick on the whole bike, one most people don't even notice, is the

windshield. If you look carefully you see the "chrome strip" that circles the police-style windshield isn't a chrome strip at all. The chrome strip and even the screw heads are actually more airbrush work from the talented Sylvain Beliveau.

With help from his fellow Canadians, Michael Ethier has built a unique Dresser. Whether it's the bright paint, the quality accessories or the fabricated parts, it all works to make one bright Harley-Davidson. A bike that Michael calls, "A real eye opener."

ABOVE The engine in Michael's Dresser displaces 80 cubic inches and is essentially stock on the inside. Outside, however, it's a different story. The engine is all polished aluminum and powder coat, which was done in four separate colors.

A "DRESSER" FROM
ARLEN NESS

Amidst all the hoopla and apparent success that now surrounds Arlen Ness it's easy to forget that he is in essence a custom motorcycle builder – one with a talent for fresh, clever designs. After more than 30 years in the business Arlen has built everything from rigid-framed Sportsters to two-wheeled Ferrari-bodied customs. Each of Arlen's machines is different from the one before, with unique features and a host of innovations.

The bikes Arlen calls his Luxury Liners started as "Convertibles" – bikes he conceived to be two bikes in one. By removing the fairing and swapping the full fenders for smaller fenders that came with the bike when it was ordered, a person could convert the bike from cruiser mode to bar hopper in an afternoon.

The trouble with the two-for-one concept lies in the success of the full-cruise mode. The bikes are so comfortable, with the fairing to keep off the bugs and the bags to provide a place to put a few necessities, that no one ever took off the full-dress outfit.

So what we have is an Arlen Ness Luxury Liner: a Convertible turned Dresser. Arlen thought that if people were using them as Dressers, why not go all the way and provide a tour pack so people can really tour on these long-legged highway bikes.

Underneath the fairing, bags and tour pack is an Arlen Ness Dyna-style frame with five inches of stretch and a 35 degree fork angle. "Dyna-style" means rubber-mounted in the fashion of the Dyna models. The frame itself is made from one and a quarter-inch mild steel tubing, though the signature twin-rail swingarm is built from chrome-moly tubing.

Though the Arlen Ness catalog is filled with the latest billet aluminum wheel designs, most of the 'Liners seem to come with spoked wheels. Specifically, a pair of 18 inch aluminum rims laced to Arlen Ness hubs. The hot setup is to install a 170X18-inch tire at the back, which actually makes for a slightly wider end result than a 180, when used with a 5-3/4 inch rim.

Bolted to the front of the frame are the billet, mid-glide triple trees from the Ness catalog clamping a pair of shortened 39mm fork tubes. At the back, two 12-1/2-inch aluminum-bodied shocks hold up the signature twin-rail swingarm.

There is no "Arlen Ness motor" (at least not yet). 80-cubic-inch Luxury Liners use mostly Harley-Davidson internal components mounted in polished S&S cases. The bike shown here uses the larger displacement option, a 96-cubic-inch polished S&S engine with Edelbrock heads, a Carl's camshaft, S&S carburetor and a two-into-one SuperTrapp/Ness exhaust.

The "96" from S&S uses the full line of in-house polished billet parts. On the right side, the cam cover, tappet blocks, pushrod covers and two-piece rocker boxes are all from the catalog. On the left, the chrome-plated outer primary carries the Arlen Ness logo. The transmission is adorned with the same kind of billet jewelry, including the top cover, and the right side cover which also houses the slave cylinder for the hydraulic clutch mechanism.

These bikes get their distinctive looks from the sleek fairing and lowers, an original Arlen Ness design. It's interesting to note that the headlight still mounts to the fork and not the fairing. Which made it possible to pull the fairing off without removing the headlight during conversion to convertible mode. Today it means the headlight turns with the fork and points the way around corners, a feature many motorcyclists have come to rely on.

Taildragger fenders do a good job of protecting the rider in any kind of inclement weather and provide the bike with nice lines. The unique bags and tour pack provide the storage needed by one or two riders out for a day or a week. Between the neck and the Danny Gray seat is the long, one piece gas tank, hand formed from sheet aluminum.

Unlike some of the stripped-down customs, these bikes come with the full complement of switches on the bars. Look closely and you find they even have turn signals, the front lights incorporated into the mirror stalk and the rears built into the fender strut.

Each of the limited production 'Liners carries a unique paint job. The purple and white paint job is the work of Arlen and Jon Nelson, with wild graphics by Carl Brouhard.

Arlen is justifiably proud of these bikes, as much for their user-friendly nature and durability as the unique design. A Luxury Liner is now Arlen's preferred ride to Sturgis each year. As he likes to explain, "We had seven of these bikes in Sturgis and we all rode back together. All the way from Sturgis to California and we had no problems whatsoever. A lot of guys who build custom bikes like to say 'we ride them,' but nobody rides them as far as that."

ABOVE Carl Brouhard is responsible for the graphics package. Turn signals are integrated into the stalks of the mirrors.

ABOVE LEFT Unique Ness bars mount the small speedo in the center. Clamps for the brake and clutch master cylinders house small switches for turn signals, horn and kill switch.

NO MORE
BAD LUCK CHARM

ABOVE Harley-Davidson Dressers tend to look better and better as owners take more and more of the visual distractions off the bike. By removing some of the lights and accessories the basic design of the bike is able to shine through.

OPPOSITE Most of the covers on this side are simple chrome covers from Harley-Davidson. Even though these use rubber-mounted engines, many riders still use cushioned floor boards to further reduce the effects of vibration.

Brian Kehoe from Bethesda, Maryland, wasn't sure the 1990 FLH was jinxed – even though the first owner had three major accidents with the bike – until he had an accident himself shortly after rebuilding the bike. "At that point," explains Brian, "I was ready to try something different. The stock bike seemed like a big bad luck charm."

Some of the changes made to the bike are more obvious than others, but the total effect is to clean up the bike without a radical change in character. After the fourth accident, Brian figured he had to disassemble and repair the bike anyway. Why not just forget to reinstall some of the parts, and swap non-stock items for others?

Most obvious among all the missing parts is the tour pack and the stock windshield. Less obvious is the missing stock turn signals for both the front and back of the big Dresser. In front, the blinkers are mounted flush at the outer edge of the factory fairing, while at the rear the turn signals are set into the lower corner of the saddle bags.

Instead of buying another Dresser fender, Brian mounted a Fat Boy front fender. By using the mounting bracket from the stock Dresser fender, he was able to get the new fender mounted down nice and close to the 16-inch Dunlop tire. The wheels are another subtle, but significant, upgrade. Brian parked the cast Dresser wheels in the corner with the tour pack and used sparkling chrome-plated spoked wheels in their place.

As long as he had everything apart, Brian reasoned it only made good sense to upgrade the motor as well. With help from his friend "Wilbur" Brian stripped the V-Twin down to bare cases and then sent

RIGHT Dressers benefit from a buffed out motor just as much as a Softail or FXR does. Note the polished cases, cylinders with missing fins, polished and painted cylinders and heads, and the polished inner and outer primary.

everything out for polish and paint. Ed's Polishing in Landover, Maryland, put a bright shine on the factory cases, took the bottom three fins off the cylinders before polishing the remaining fins, and also shined up the fins on the Harley heads.

The engine upgrade included a fresh valve job for the heads, high-compression Wiseco pistons for the cylinders, and stock Harley components inside the engine cases. An Andrews camshaft and adjustable pushrods take the place of stock components, while a Super E carburetor from S&S with matching air cleaner takes the place of the Keihin CV carburetor. Most of the engine covers are simple chrome-plated components from Harley-Davidson though Brian did opt for billet lifter blocks and pushrod tubes from Arlen Ness. On the right side a two-into-one Thunderheader takes the place of the stock Harley-Davidson exhaust system.

Most people agree the stock five-speed transmission will stand up to all but the worst abuse. Brian agrees and settled for a simple inspection and rebuild, with back-cut gears for easier shifting. Unlike the engine cases, the transmission case is painted to match the rest of the machine.

Final sheet metal improvements include an extended rear fender and a mildly stretched stock gas tank with matching dash. All the sheet metal modifications are the handiwork of Bart Poole, the same man who customized the fairing and bags.

Having strayed considerably from stock, Brian couldn't foresee painting the bike in stock colors. Instead Preston Doyle from Doyle's Customs applied kandy brandywine from the House of Kolor and then did the unusual and very colorful graphics. Even the seat, made special for the bike by John Longo of Rockville, Maryland, is stitched in colors that match the kandy paint job. After masking off the fins, Preston used the same shade of kolorful kandy to paint both the cylinders and heads.

At the very end of the project, Brian and Bart did a bit more parts swapping. The fork utilizes fork tubes one inch shorter than stock and the front brakes use chrome-plated factory calipers. To match the drop in the front height, White Brothers shock absorber brackets are used to lower the back of the bike.

Now, more than two years after the "final" reassembly, Brian is still riding the big FLH, with no loss of paint or skin, and no unplanned meetings with other vehicles. The long string of bad luck is broken. When it's time to ride, Brian simply turns the key, the Thunderheader barks and the bright candy Dresser rolls out of the driveway and down the road.

ABOVE The nice deep color is kandy brandywine from House of Kolor. Graphics might fall into the currently popular "tribal" category. Tribal or not, they are very, very bright.

A POLICE CRUISER
TURNED CUSTOM HARLEY

ABOVE The Taildragger fenders add to the extreme low-ness of this ride until the bike seems to almost merge with the asphalt. Like most Baggers, this one looks good with dual exhaust.

The bikes we call "Dressers" come in various forms, everything from Road King to Ultra Hog. The bike seen here started life as a police bike, complete with fairing, extra lights and saddle bags with the big round release knobs on top.

Doug Daniel from Wellington, Texas, found the bike as a wreck. But before buying the machine he called his old friend Terry McConnell to see if Terry could help him create something interesting based on the old police bike.

As Terry tells the story, "Doug called and asked, 'could I do anything with a Dresser?' I said, 'You bet!, I'll show you what we can do with a Dresser.'" Terry goes on to explain that most of his two-wheeled projects are pro-street bikes (see Terry's hardtail in Chapter 4) so he took on Doug's Dresser partly as a personal challenge.

The planning part of the project occurred in a restaurant, where Doug started sketching ideas on a napkin. Pretty soon Terry took over and sketched out a very low, sleek Bagger that Doug really liked. Back at the shop Terry did a detailed rendering with a long gas tank, rounded tops to the bags and an interesting color scheme. "I decided we should build a real clean bike," explains Terry. "A tasteful custom, something that wouldn't look dated right away."

The sophistication of Terry's design starts at the very front of the bike where an Arlen Ness fender wraps around the 18 inch Metzeler tire and extends almost all the way to the asphalt. Just above the fender the headlight is mounted in a Road King headlight nacelle. The gas tank, based on the original, seems to start pretty far forward on the frame and then extends all the way back to the side covers. The

two-tone color scheme that begins at the headlight nacelle runs across the gas tank and continues across the saddle bags. The bags themselves are capped with the fiberglass covers with a shape intended to mimic that of the rear fender.

To convert this one-time pursuit vehicle Terry asked Steve Stonez to stretch the frame four inches and increase the rake to 40 degrees. Little things make a big difference here, in this case the frame was raked and extended in such a way that the neck actually moved closer to the front gas tank mount. "I didn't want to see a big hunk of square tubing between the neck and the front of the gas tank," explains Terry. "We made sure the front of the tank came up very close to the steering neck."

Bob at Carefree Highway Truckin' in Tulsa extended the tank, again to Terry McConnell's specific instructions. "I didn't just want the tank extended," says Terry. "I wanted the back of the tank to wrap around the front of the seat, and the tails to extend down and almost merge with the side covers."

The small seat is the work of Eric Long, Terry's right hand man, who also did much of the assembly of the sleek former police bike. The covers for the saddle bags, however, are part of Doug's contribution to the project. Between the saddle bags is another Arlen Ness tail-dragger fender equipped with a trick LED taillight designed and installed by Doug and Eric.

Though the body work and paint, done mostly by the "Dough Boy," takes center stage; Doug and Terry didn't exactly skimp when it came time to choose the right hardware. The Pro One billet wheels measure 18 inches on both ends. The front tire is a 140/70X18 while the back is a 150/70X18.

For brakes the crew decided to stay with a simple theme. Both front and rear brakes use single factory-style calipers coupled with stainless-steel rotors designed to match the wheels.

In spite of the fact that the engine in Doug's new bike was in pretty good shape, a little warm up seemed to be in order. For a boost in compression, A.M. Lewinskie from Tulsa installed a pair of Wiseco 10.5 to 1 pistons, a Crane camshaft and an S&S Super E carburetor. The air cleaner cover from Sumax adds style, as do the Bartels mufflers and the Pro One billet engine covers.

Terry has a theory about how low a bike should be, "If it doesn't drag when you back it out of the shop, roll it back in and fix it." Thus the final assembly included a White Brothers lowering kit in the front fork and shorter shocks at the back.

From black and white, Doug's cruiser has gone to black and sandstone. A former pursuit vehicle now being pursued at every event by photographers and onlookers. All of whom want to know, "where'd you get the covers for the saddle bags, how long is that gas tank, and how in the world did you get it that low?"

ABOVE In the wind, Doug and his partner at speed in Nevada.

ABOVE LEFT Terry's clever sheet metal design and paint make for a very appealing bike that doesn't use much of the standard billet jewelry.